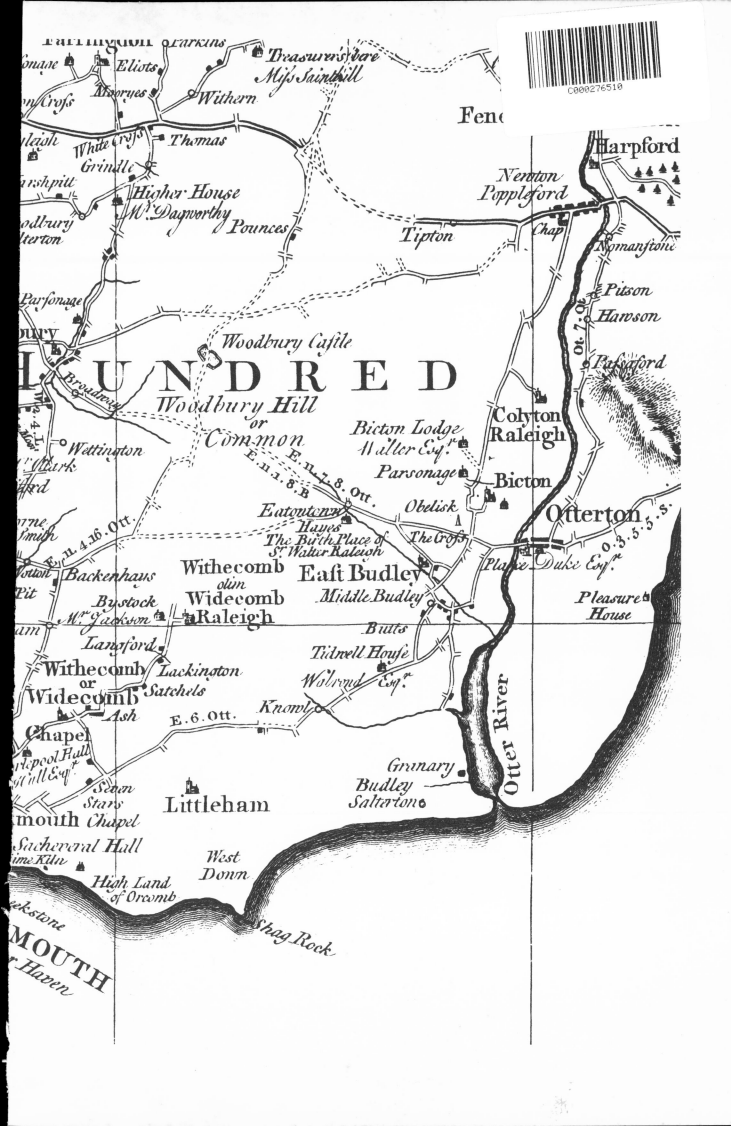

THE BOOK OF EXMOUTH

FRONT COVER: The first Holy Trinity Church on Chapel Hill, 1772,
by C. W. Bampfylde. Not a single building in sight survives. (EL)

Holy Trinity Church, 1906, with its builders. (WG)

THE BOOK OF EXMOUTH

PORTRAIT OF A RESORT

BY

ROBIN BUSH

BARRACUDA BOOKS LIMITED
BUCKINGHAM, ENGLAND
MCMLXXVIII

PUBLISHED BY BARRACUDA BOOKS LIMITED

BUCKINGHAM, ENGLAND

AND PRINTED BY

FRANK ROOK LIMITED

TOWER BRIDGE ROAD

LONDON SE1

BOUND BY

BOOKBINDERS OF LONDON LIMITED

LONDON N5

JACKET PRINTED BY

WHITE CRESCENT PRESS LIMITED

LUTON, ENGLAND

LITHOGRAPHY BY

SOUTH MIDLANDS LITHOPLATES LIMITED

LUTON, ENGLAND

DISPLAY TYPE SET IN

MONOTYPE BASKERVILLE SERIES 169

BY SOUTH BUCKS TYPESETTERS LIMITED

BEACONSFIELD, ENGLAND

TEXT SET IN 12/14PT BASKERVILLE

BY BEAVER REPROGRAPHICS LIMITED

BUSHEY, ENGLAND

ISBN 0 86023 057 0

Contents

Acknowledgements

In this account of the town where I spent my formative years, I have tried, on a limited canvas, to show how Exmouth began and how it grew. This is *not* the history of Littleham and Withycombe Raleigh, although these two places are inevitably part of the story. As far as possible I have tried not merely to duplicate, but to complement the work of others and to introduce fresh material drawn from hitherto unused sources. For all omissions and opinions I hold myself responsible.

I am particularly indebted to my friend, Ian Cann, who has unselfishly allowed me free access to his work. The abstracting of Exmouth material from Exeter newspapers, a project he undertook at my suggestion many years ago, he has carried to a triumphant conclusion. My thanks also to Bill Gorfin, that eternal Exmothian, for his constant willingness to share with me his store of information.

This work owes a considerable debt for both its illustrations and publicity to Devon County Libraries, to the County Librarian, Rex Charlesworth, and to his staff. I have had free access to the collections of pictures held at the Thomas Abell reference library in Exmouth and the West Country Studies library in Exeter. I have also made full use of the remarkable collection of Exmouth photographs amassed by Leslie Hill and Nigel Batten. Over many years I have received help and guidance at the Devon Record Office and Exeter Cathedral Library and from their archivists, particularly Miss Joan Sinar, Mrs Audrey Erskine, Mrs Margery Rowe, Michael Dickinson and Trevor Falla.

Two writers have considerably influenced this present work: firstly, Eric Delderfield, who has chronicled the history of the town with great affection. His books first stimulated my interest in Exmouth's past and, in particular, it would be hard to improve upon his account of the last century. Secondly, Dr E. A. G. Clark's history of the Exe estuary and its economy has guided my thinking in many respects. Where I have unearthed fresh information, it has almost invariably borne out his conclusions.

Among many others who have assisted me in different ways, I must mention Bob Britton, Geoffrey Paley, Lawrence Saunders and Mrs Hilda Moorhouse. To my publisher, Clive Birch, for his impatience to receive my text and for his sympathetic treatment of my work, my gratitude. Finally, to my parents, who have done so much to promote this book, and to my wife, for putting up with me and my notes during its writing, my thanks.

EXMOUTH.
May 1978.

Dedication

To my parents, who introduced me to Exmouth
26 years ago—and have made it their home.

Foreword

by the Rt Hon Lord Clinton JP

It is a great pleasure to me to write a foreword to Robin Bush's excellent publication *The Book of Exmouth*, particularly as my family have had connections with the town for many years, and have been Lords of the Manor of Littleham since the sixteenth century.

Robin Bush's research from earliest times to the present day has produced a most interesting book, and he has a fascinating story to tell. The author has made excellent use of the many pictures which illustrate his text.

I know that the reader of this book will find it of varied interest, and historically it is an account of the development of a town which has made use of its location beside the sea and on the estuary of the Exe, illustrating the trade which has taken place in shipping and fishing as well as the watering place of Hanoverian times.

This most valuable work will make an excellent addition to any bookshelf.

Preface

by Cllr D. E. Dray, Chairman of Exmouth Town Committee

Mr Robin Bush, a professional historian and archivist who was brought up in Exmouth, has taken a new look at the history of our town, the oldest resort in the south-west. For the first time, the Rolle estate records and Exeter City archives have been used to illuminate the origins of the small village at its heart. He has shown how it developed around the ferry-station in Exeter Road, eventually swallowing up the older villages of Littleham and Withycombe Raleigh.

The growth of the watering place, which boasted the first known swimming bath in the south-west, is recounted with human stories of the innkeepers, the smugglers, the rich and the poor.

Using contemporary newspaper accounts, the author tells the story with warmth and affection for his former home. His illustrations, the majority never before published, depict many facets of the town's life and the way in which it has changed over the years.

Ode addressed to the Bathing Machines at Exmouth

Far from th'ignoble tribe, I silent hail
Th'amphibious buildings of this sea-clos'd vale,
Temples of health! which grace Exmothia's shore!
Sole sovereigns ye of these wide watry fields!
To whom the sea her daily tribute yields
Of coral shells and wild fantastic ore:
        Your priestesses each early morn
        Salute the fragrant brine,
        While in your sacred robes of snow
        Fair nymphs their limbs entwine,
And beauty from your portals wide re-ushers more divine.

The blustering winter your low roofs defy,
While howling whirlwinds whistle wildly by,
And foaming surges sweep the sounding shore,
Whose curling summits dare the low'ring cloud,
White eddying sand is whisk'd on blasts aloud,
And repercussive rocks return the roar.
        Still, amid nature's wreck secure,
        You view the scene forlorn,
        And while the stout, the towering mast,
        Is crackling downward borne,
Your sacred humble roofs nor dread, nor yet provoke, the storm.

Oft as your hallow'd rounds I silent tread,
As fancy holds sweet converse with the dead,
From yon rough rocks, upon th'enraptur'd sight
Bursts the pale moon in silver majesty,
And in the bosom of the tranquil sea
Pours her broad stream of pure refulgent light:
        The winds their hollow breath retain,
        Unheard the minutes veer,
        Unruffled floats the azure main,
        No voice, no sound is near,
Save where some hapless lover's sigh slow undulates the air.

From *The Gentleman's Magazine*, July 1783.

At the Mouth of the Exe

Exmouth is the oldest resort in the County of Devon. For over two and a half centuries men and women have come here in search of health and contentment — since the days when resorts were known as watering places. But in other respects Exmouth is a comparatively youthful settlement. In origin, it was a mediaeval fishing village which developed around a ferry-station on the boundary between the two Saxon parishes of Littleham and Withycombe Raleigh. It lay almost surrounded by agricultural Devonshire, a landscape of scattered farms and hamlets, its ownership dominated at first by the Church and later by the Rolles of Bicton and the Hulls of Marpool.

Gradually during the 18th century, Exmothians became accustomed to the periodic influx of strangers, began to realise that in the sea which gave them fish and often snatched away their lives they held an unexploited treasure. The rich, the titled and the famous came, at first from Exeter and then from further afield. Inns, lodging-houses and eventually hotels sprang up to house them. They in turn built houses, villas and mansions. For over a century Exmouth's 'golden age' continued, until the railway opened up Dawlish, Teignmouth and finally Torquay. And it was Torquay's rise which marked Exmouth's gradual decline as a fashionable watering place. But the town did not die: after years of planning and frustration, it too achieved its own railway and docks. It became a port and, with its two miles of golden sands, a resort for the family, a retirement town and to some extent a dormitory for Exeter.

There are other sides to Exmouth's story: the fishermen, pilots and lifeboatmen who braved the elements to bring sustenance and safety to its people; the smugglers and revenue men who fought a running battle along its shores; the laceworkers who laboured for a pittance and lived in grinding poverty behind the glossy facade which the town showed to its visitors. Today it betrays no trace of its mediaeval origins. It is a modern town, not over-commercialised, but one which has largely forgotten its remoter past.

Early on a winter's morning, it is still possible for a man to turn his back upon a thriving town and stand on a tide-washed beach. He can gaze over a limitless sea and, as the wind whips the sand into his face, imagine those days when Exmouth was unthought of: a time when only a few cottages and a name, Pratteshide, gave a hint of what was to come.

ABOVE: Littleham village, 1890. (LHNB) BELOW: Withycombe village,
the original settlement of Bradham manor, with St Michael's Chapel,
1805. (LHNB)

12

Pratteshide

Some few miles east of the Exe estuary rises a long barren ridge, Woodbury Common, taking its name from the double-banked earthen fort or camp which crowns it. The 'woodbeorh', built about four thousand years ago, may have witnessed the last resistance in this area to the spread of the mighty Roman Empire. Only twelve miles from the mouth of the river stands Exeter, the cantonal capital of the Dumnonii, the tribe of ancient Britons who occupied this land before it fell under the hand of the legions. The Romans built roads, but long before their network was completed, and even after, many of the goods vital to the life of such a city must have been brought upriver to be unloaded at Topsham and carried overland to Exeter's gates.

Roman coins have indeed been unearthed at Exmouth: one of Hadrian (AD117-138) near Boarden Barn and another of Crispus (AD317-326), minted at Lyons in France, but there is no evidence that the Romans ever settled here. A look-out or signal station may have been built to take advantage of Exmouth's strategic position, but if so, all trace of it is lost. The earliest hint of permanent settlement comes in the 11th century name for the Point, Lydwicnaesse, meaning the ness or promontory of the Lidwiccas, as the Saxons called the Bretons. It suggests the presence of a former British hamlet possibly deserted by its inhabitants because of its exposed position.

This corner of south-east Devon lay within the hundred of East Budleigh. The hundred was a Saxon subdivision of the county with its own court, and East Budleigh may have been the first Saxon settlement in the area. The oldest and largest estate in the vicinity of modern Exmouth was the manor of Littleham which, like the rest of the hundred, was retained by the kings of Wessex until the 11th century. In 1042 King Edward the Confessor gave half a manse or hide of land at Littleham, together with a wood on its southern side, probably less than 100 acres of land, to his thegn or minister, Ordgar. The small area of the grant indicates how much of the manor was then unsettled and uncultivated. With minor variations, the boundaries of the land given mark out the modern parish of Littleham, following the stream which used to run down Margaret Street and a ridgeway heading north-east towards Budleigh Salterton, and mentioning a crossroads where Capel Lane now joins Salterton Road. Of the names recorded, only Auanford on the Withycombe Brook survived into modern times as Eaverds Brake. The wood may well have been the same which was partly cleared for the settlement of the manor or farm of Wode or Wood, later Woodlands Farm. The site of Littleham was well inland, the centre of an agricultural and not a fishing community, relatively secure from raids on the river's mouth.

It was probably Ordgar's son, the giant Ordulf, who gave Littleham to the monastery of Horton in East Dorset, where he asked to be buried. When Horton was transferred to Sherborne Abbey in 1139, Littleham manor went with it, and continued in the hands of the monks there until the abbey's dissolution by Henry VIII. It was a considerable property. In

1086 Domesday recorded 15 smallholders and 20 cottagers there, and it had nearly 100 tenants in 1388. In 1540 Littleham, together with the hundred of East Budleigh, was sold to Sir Thomas Dennys and with the manor of Bicton descended through his granddaughter Anne to the Rolle family and eventually to the Barons Clinton. The Clinton estate, created over nine centuries ago, still includes much of the southern area of modern Exmouth. The former manor house evidently stood immediately north of Littleham Church until the 19th century and was known as Lord's House.

Within Littleham, the later farms of Liverton and Woodlands had been converted to freehold by the 14th century and together became the manor of Wode *iuxta* (near) Chickstone. The estate was held in the 15th century by the Raleighs of Nettlecombe, Somerset; it descended to the Trevelyans and was acquired by the Rolles, after the death of Thomas Trevelyan of Liverton in 1740, to become once more part of Littleham manor. Spratshayes, its house dating from an 18th century rebuilding after a fire, was another early freehold and farm of Littleham, probably bought from Sherborne Abbey by the Crockers of Lyneham in the 15th century and held under them by John Drake. His son, Gilbert Drake, purchased it under an undischarged mortgage of 1542. It descended to the Fords of Nutwell and Holwells of Woodbury and was carried back to the Drakes by marriage. The last of that name to live there, the Rev Edward Holwell Drake, died in 1797, and his widow sold the farm to John Drew in 1803. From Drew's nephew, Henry Pratt, it eventually passed to his great-granddaughter, who left it in the present century to the National Trust.

To the north of Littleham and again well inland lay the manor of Withycombe, centred on St John's Church and the present Withycombe Barton, the site of the former manor house. It was held at the Norman Conquest by a Saxon woman, Alveva, but William I granted it to Walter de Claville, from whose descendants it became known as Withycombe Claville. By 1273 the Clavilles had sublet the manor to Sir Hugh Raleigh, whose family held it from the priory of Canonsleigh, founded by the Clavilles, for the rent of a pair of white gloves or ½d a year. The Raleighs, including the father of the famous Sir Walter, occupied the estate for at least three centuries and their name displaced that of the Clavilles as the suffix which it bears to this day. It was evidently purchased by the illegitimate descendants of Sir Walter's elder brother George, and passed thence through Sir Nicholas Hooper (died 1731) to his son-in-law, John Bassett, MP, after whom Bassett Park and Bassett's Farm were named. Bassett sold the manor in 1756 to William Jackson and it eventually passed by sale to Edward Divett in 1801 and continued to be held by the owners of Bystock until 1911.

West of Withycombe, towards the river, lay Bradham, the 'broad ham' as distinct from the 'little ham'. The men of Bradham contributed 26s 8d towards the marriage of the king's daughter in 1167, and by 1189 the land of Bradham was rented by St Nicholas' Priory in Exeter. King John granted the manor of Bradham to the priory in 1204, and its property was soon after increased by a rent of 6s 8d from land in Halisdon (Halsdon) given by Roger de Claville, and again in 1316 by the grant of Isenelonde (later known as Island, south of Courtlands) by Roger of Babbeton (Bapton). Inevitably, St Nicholas' Priory also fell under the hand of Henry VIII, who in 1539 leased the manor for life to Philip Dennys and in 1557 let Marepole (Marpool) and Bapton to his brother Thomas Dennys. However, the freehold of the manor was sold, also in 1557, to John Drake of Ash and his son Barnard, and later passed through the families of Raymond and Rodde to the Hulls of Marpool. What is today known as Withycombe village represents the original settlement of the men of Bradham. Marpool Hall was bought by Sir John Phear (died 1905) and demolished in

1951. Phear Park was given to the town by the Phear family in 1909.

A broad strip of waste land along the boundary of Withycombe with Lympstone seems to have belonged to the Courtenays, Earls of Devon, possibly as lords of East Budleigh hundred. It was known in 1219 as Holham, sometimes as Haldeham or Holdeham, now Hulham, and the manor was forfeited to the Crown on the execution of Henry Courtenay, Marquis of Exeter, in 1539. Acquired by the Drakes in 1549, half was used by Robert Drake to endow a charity in 1628; the other half passed through a variety of hands to John Drew Pratt of Spratshayes, being split up and sold after his death in 1910.

Bystock, an 'island' of land which belonged to the parish and manor of Colaton Raleigh as long ago as 1086, was given by Henry I to an ancestor of Nicholas de Meriet in exchange for Topsham manor and was subsequently granted to Polsloe Priory. After the Priory's dissolution it was sold in 1546 to the covetous Drakes and conveyed by them to William Jackson in 1742, who still held it in 1773. Twenty years later it was sold by one Mr Day to Henry Cutler, who conveyed Bystock in about 1800 to Edward Divett (died 1819). After the death of Divett's son, Edward, MP, it was bought by the Bryces of Marley in 1872, and by F. C. Hunter in 1906. While being redecorated for Mr Hunter in the latter year, it was burnt down. Rebuilt by Hunter with 67 rooms, it was acquired by Major C. P. Bradshaw in 1935, and his widow sold it to a Christian association which has run it as a community refuge since 1965.

None of these early estates formed the nucleus of the modern Exmouth, for it was a small property within the manor of Bradham which was to give birth to a little fishing village and later a resort. In the 12th century a man called Robert Uppehille lived on the western slopes of what is now Marpool Hill and from which he took his name. His son Morin appears to have served as the king's bailiff for East Budleigh hundred when Bradham manor was granted to St Nicholas' Priory, and his lands were specifically excepted from that grant. This small estate was bounded to the west by the present Exeter Road and then the sea shore, to the north by Withycombe Road, to the east by Marpool Hill and to the south by Margaret Street. Morin's descendants continued to hold the land in return for acting as hundred bailiff or beadle. His daughter, Maisanta, brought it to her husband Geoffrey, who in turn took the name Uppehille or de la Hulle, 'of the hill'. Their male line ended on the death of John Depe or Dupe in the late 14th century, when the estate was divided between the families of his aunts Sokespiche of Marsh Barton in Clyst St George and Cole. John Drake bought out their interests between 1526 and 1528 and, later known as the manor of Hille alias Rull or Rill, the land passed through the Raymonds to the Hulls of Marpool.

In 1302 there were a manor house and three cottages on this land but by 1482 40 houses had been built there. This rapid growth can be traced to a hamlet centred on a small plot of land on the foreshore, measuring 55 yards by 37 yards. Morin had granted this land to John the miller in about 1240, and it was bought soon after by the Mayor and citizens of Exeter for use as a ferry-station. It was then known as Pratteshuthe, later Pratteshide, meaning Pratt's landing place, and it was the site known in more modern times as Mona Island in Exeter Road, which now accommodates public conveniences in front of Glenorchy Church. Such was Exmouth's prosaic beginning.

The city of Exeter claimed to control the river estuary as far as a rock called Orcheston and later Chickstone. Similar rights over both the estuary and its fishery were claimed by the Earls of Devon and, in respect of Littleham manor, by Sherborne Abbey. In 1265-6 Exeter and Sherborne agreed that all rights in the ferry, described as 'the passage of the

15

water of Checkston', would in future belong to the city, in return for which the abbot, monks, their horses, carriages and goods would be conveyed free of charge and the monks permitted to fish in the river and buy and sell fish at Littleham. Presumably the original departure point for the ferry lay in Littleham and was transferred to Withycombe by the Mayor and citizens of Exeter when they bought the quay at Pratteshide. That same ferry still leaves Exmouth to cross the estuary as it did over seven centuries ago.

The Exmouth area c1805.

ABOVE: Domesday Book, 1086. Littleham in the hands of Horton Priory; Withycombe Raleigh held by Walter de Claville. CENTRE: Bassett's Farm, Withycombe, named after John Bassett, lord of the manor. BELOW: Grant by John Uppehull to the Mayor of Exeter of two messuages in Bradham, next Littleham, 1327. (ECM)

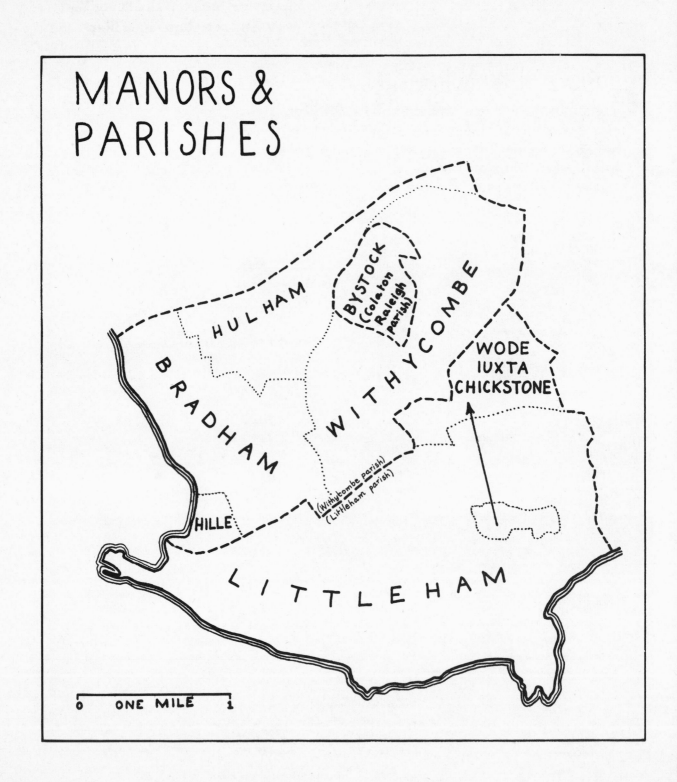

MANORS & PARISHES

HULHAM

BYSTOCK
(Colaton Raleigh parish)

WITHYCOMBE

WODE IUXTA CHICKSTONE

BRADHAM

(Withycombe parish)
(Littleham parish)

HILLE

LITTLEHAM

0   ONE MILE   1

18

ABOVE: Front view of Bystock House, the seat of Edward Divett MP, burnt 1906. (LHNB) CENTRE: Marpool Hall, demolished 1951, (LHNB) and BELOW: the entrance gates and lodge to Marpool Hall, now the gateway to Phear Park. (LHNB)

19

ABOVE: Hulham House, 1911. BELOW: Exmouth from the Hulham
Road, 1829. (EL)

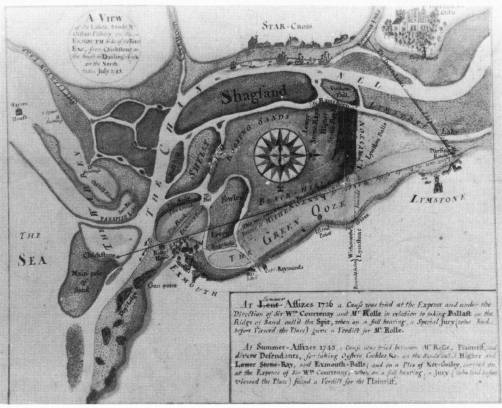

ABOVE: Traditional manor house of Rill, North Street. (EL) BELOW:
Map of the Exe estuary, 1743. (EL)

21

ABOVE: Grant by John de Molendino (the miller) to the Mayor of Exeter
of a house at Pratteshide, c1250. (ECM) BELOW: Grant by Mariota,
widow of John de Molendino, to the Mayor of Exeter of a tenement in
Pratteshide, 1268. (ECM)

22

Withyn the Haven Mouth

The size and importance of Exmouth in mediaeval times have been much exaggerated. The claim that a settlement here was burnt by the Danes when they raided this part of the coast in 1001 is not referred to by the contemporary Anglo-Saxon Chronicle and only turns up in much later accounts. The name Exmouth was used to describe the port of Exeter and the creeks of the estuary, the city's jurisdiction extending beyond the Chickstone Rock 'as far as a humber barrel can be descried'; the site of the later town was at first known as either Pratteshide or Chickstone. The ten ships contributed to Edward III's Calais expedition in 1346 and which still sail sedately across the town's coat of arms were contributed by Exeter with its dependent ports, and not by the growing hamlet behind the Point.

The truth is that as far as we can tell, the main channel seems always to have clung to the western side of the estuary and boats could only approach the ferry-station quay up a shallow creek. Until the 19th century, most vessels had to tranship their cargo to the shore by lighters. The control of the estuary by the Mayor of Exeter was absolute; captains had to seek permission before they were allowed to land goods anywhere other than Topsham, and town dues continued to be paid to Exeter for such landings even after Exmouth docks were built in 1865. Licences to discharge at Pratteshide are recorded in the Mayor's court rolls, but they were granted only infrequently. Thus in 1290 David Uppehille claimed unsuccessfully that the water of Pratteshide belonged to his manor of Hille, and in 1343 Adam Dally of Seaton paid 6s 8d to unload 20 quarters of salt and the like amount of corn there. Similarly, in 1365 a ship of 140 tons called the *George* of Exmouth, belonging to an Exeter merchant, Roger Plente, was too large to discharge at Topsham and had licence to unload at the unidentified Colepole nearby.

The shallow water at the quay was not the only factor which inhibited the growth of the settlement. The cost and difficulties of transporting goods inland from Exmouth were considerable at a time when the road system was in its infancy. In 1387 the way from Exeter to Chickstone was obstructed by the parson of Lympstone, who dug trenches across it 'where men and cattle of those parts have been wont to pass', and the hundred court rolls show that on one occasion it took at least three years, between 1453 and 1456, to get a highway repaired at 'Redsloe' in Littleham. The vulnerability of the anchorage led to sea defence works at an early date. In 1545 Woodbury churchwardens contributed 13s 4d 'to the makyng of the bullworks at Exmouthe by Chekystone and yn the Meyre' (Maer). The works at the Point probably consisted of a bank known as the Dam which was raised to prevent the sea breaking over the Point (then only a sandbank) and sinking fishing boats anchored in its lee.

The passage or ferry station continued to be the principal attraction, bringing strangers and their money to Pratteshide's shores. In 1287 Exeter leased it to John Pycard for 44s a year, on condition that he maintained the ferry house and boat. The evident success of the enterprise prompted Sherborne Abbey vainly to contest Exeter's rights in 1348, 1412 and

23

1473. The rising fortunes of the Drake family, substantial landowners after the Dissolution, led John Drake to take a lease of the lucrative ferry in 1542, together with Pratteshide quay, then measuring 100 ft by 80 ft. The name of the quay evidently inspired the name of the Drake family home near Littleham village, now called Spratshayes but formerly known as Pratteshead alias Pratteshayes. The Drakes continued to run the ferry until 1624, employing ferrymen such as William Helion, mentioned in 1603. Under the Watts family, lessees between 1625 and 1686, the passage boat was wrecked on 4 September 1633 and three men drowned. The body of one, William Walter, was not found for over a month and the parish register comments that he was, wisely enough, buried 'in ye sand'.

The profits of the official ferryman were constantly threatened by rival boatmen, and efforts to prevent such activities were made in 1634, 1745 and 1748. Excessive fares charged by the ferrymen constituted another headache for the Exeter Corporation, which imposed a fixed scale of tolls in the late 18th century, and irregular attendance at the ferry station was also remarked on in 1774. During the second half of the 18th century a new passage house was built on the point; the old quay fell into disuse and was finally cut off from the river by an embankment built by William Thomas Hull, along which the railway now runs.

In its new position, the ferry station was more vulnerable. It was damaged by winds and high tides in 1796 and 1815, and in 1817 was totally washed away. Under new ferry charges introduced in 1838, each passenger was to pay 2d, every horse 4d; carriages with two wheels paid 1s, four wheels 1s 6d, and if drawn by more than one horse 3s. All tolls were doubled after sunset. The service was viewed with distaste by some and fear by others. One of many critics described in 1843 how, when carriages were transported, two wheels hung in the air over one side of the boat, balanced by large stones hung over the other. Only a year later, the Exeter Corporation was no doubt quite relieved to dispose of the ferry to the South Devon Railway Company for £1,000. Then as now, the ferry probably landed at Starcross, but there was also a a service to the Warren by 1797. In 1862 the ferryman, Trim, was suspected of murdering a passenger on the Warren for his money and was only cleared when the unfortunate traveller was found drowned with his wallet intact. Today the ferry is still run by the railways.

Although Littleham ceased to control the ferry in the 13th century, its inhabitants retained the right to take fish in the river and at sea, although challenged from time to time by the Earls of Devon, as when fishermen who took up a catch near Chickstone in 1517 were prosecuted in the hundred court. To Leland in about 1540, Exmouth was 'a fisschar tounlet a little withyn the haven mouth', and in its early years the village's economy must have depended principally on fishing. Once again, poor communication with Exeter prevented the trade from having much more than local significance.

Of similar importance were the mussel, oyster and cockle beds within the shelter of the estuary. In 1566 it was ordered that the Exmouth mussel beds should not be 'broken' before Holyrood Day (14 September) and the oyster beds not before St Bartholomew's Day (24 August) and that no one should take any of 'the greatest oysters and leve the lytle byhynde'. But Exmothians have never taken kindly to authority and in the same year three fishermen were fined for breaking the mussel beds at dead of night, as was John Parker of Lympstone in 1570. Illegal nets were in use in 1578 and at times fishing tactics were even more exotic. In 1583 Leonard Morley and two others set out at night to the west of Chickstone 'disguised with sirplises or sheyites (sheets) upon their goarments, eyther to take away some other mans fysshe from their takell or to do some other unlawfull thing'. Littleham's manorial

24

rights had also to be protected from 'foreigners'; Susannah Wood of Starcross was fined in 1738 for raking cockles on Fowley, and men of Starcross, Lympstone and Withycombe in 1743 for dredging oysters on the sandbanks called Lympstone Lake, Higher and Lower Stone Ray, Exmouth Balls and Shag Sand.

The 16th century also saw the expansion of the Newfoundland fishing trade, which dominated the activities of many of the smaller south-western ports. Between 1563 and 1600 twenty-six Exmouth vessels were engaged in the Newfoundland fishery, the largest being the *Bartholomew* of 90 tons. The list also included John Whitbourne's ship the *Mayflower,* her master probably related to one of Exmouth's most famous sons. Richard Whitbourne, born at Exmouth, died 1635, was 'a traveler and adventurer into foreign countries' at the age of 15, and in 1588 equipped a ship to fight the Spanish Armada at his own expense. In 1622 he published his *Discourse and Discovery of New-found-land* and was knighted by James I shortly afterwards.

The path of commerce inevitably had its pitfalls. In 1666 Henry Ford of Nutwell wrote of the poverty in the town and begged for a reduction of county taxes, as thirty people, the wives and children of seamen impressed into the Navy, had come to the parish officers for relief. In 1718 Henry Peardon, master of a Newfoundland vessel, could still describe how he used to land his share of the transatlantic catch at Exmouth, but the continual impressment of men for the Royal Navy and a general shortage of sailors led to a decline in the trade. In 1755 Dean Milles commented that the town had 'formerly a large trade to Newfoundland, now quite lost'. Four former commanders of Newfoundland vessels died here between 1792 and 1815, and as late as 1856 Captain Bricknell of Exmouth was washed overboard on the Newfoundland cod banks, the fifth member of his immediate family to die by drowning.

Fishing expanded after communication problems were solved overnight by the arrival of the railway in 1861. Unfortunately, an attempt to reintroduce oysters to the Bight in 1867 was frustrated when sand washed from the Warren buried the shellfish. By 1869, 58 small boats were registered, engaged largely in crabbing, hooking and drifting, as also were four trawlers, and by 1883 a total of 369 Exmouth men were employed in the trade. At the close of the century, W. R. Redway established a wholesale fish business with export markets for crabs and lobsters in France and herrings for the home market. The French import tariffs on fish, introduced in 1920, killed the Redway business within three years and Exmouth's fishery declined, in common with those of other south-western ports.

Apart from fishing, pilotage was the other traditional occupation. In 1545 Sir John Russell was informed that the 'manner and turn' of the channel meant that no strange vessel could negotiate it without a pilot, and in 1573 a pilot was sentenced by the High Court of Admiralty for his negligence in losing the *John* of Lympstone by causing it 'to strike upon the sands and rocks of the sea'. As controller of the estuary, the Exeter Corporation provided twelve 'able and sufficient pylotts' in 1687, ordered all ships of more than 5 ft draught to take a pilot and agreed to build a tower on Chickstone Rock to aid navigation. When the improvement of various ports was considered in 1698, Exmouth was dismissed because of the rocks and shoals, continuing for over a mile, which 'divide the water into various and broken channels and difficult passages and seems (*sic*) insuperable to any ordinary use'. The reputation of the pilots in the 18th and 19th centuries was not of the best; a customs collector in 1806 claimed that 'several vessels have been purposely run on shore by the pilots in consequence of the masters resisting the exorbitant demands made upon them'.

Primitive methods of marking the path of the channel through the sandbanks included 'booms, beacons, posts, or trees' fixed in the sandbanks or along the shoreline. In 1816 five buoys were placed on or near the Bar and an additional charge of 1d per ton on all cargoes entering the estuary was made; in 1829 the channel from the Bar to Topsham was buoyed. The first buoy marking the entrance to the channel was known in 1843, as now, as the Fairway buoy. The rates of pilotage were fixed by Exeter Corporation, but even so those charged on the Exe in 1884 were among the highest in the kingdom. In the long term, these surcharges on the cost of cargoes led to a reduction in the use of the estuary by larger vessels and to the decline of its ports.

It was the lack of a deep-water harbour which long prevented the development of a substantial port at the mouth of the Exe. An area called 'the Docke' was mentioned at the estuary mouth in 1576, but no move to construct a permanent facility was made until 1825, when a pier at the Point was suggested, to connect with an abortive railway scheme. An Act for a similar railway project with docks at the Point was proposed in 1835 and another dock bill was actually passed in 1841. However, no progress was made until 1861, when the railway opened and plans were drawn up for a dock south-west of the station. In 1862 a proposed pier was not built, but a public meeting was held in 1863 to revive interest in a dock. In January 1865 Messrs Jackson of London started work on a natural hollow in the Point called variously Shellpit, Sleepers Bay or Dead Mans Bay. A jetty was built to unload materials and, despite a fight among the navvies because one of their number was working too hard, the new dock accommodated its first ships in 1868. The original plan for three lock gates was abandoned and only one pair was built.

The dock had a chequered career in its early days. Sixty feet of the west wall were destroyed in a gale in 1874, and two years later a vessel cut the jetty in two. The dock's use was slight at first: between 1866 and 1884 the town dues paid to Exeter were less than half of Topsham's and much less than those collected at Exeter itself. Improvements carried out in 1882-3 enabled timber ships to enter, although most cargoes comprised bulky goods of low value: coal, stone, cement, timber and slate. Messrs Sharp had timber yards there by 1883 and Messrs Wilson by 1893. The docks also served a considerable hinterland as far afield as Axmouth, and in 1894 the Dock Company, reformed in 1891, opposed the Budleigh Salterton railway because a quarter of its income was derived from trade with that town.

In 1891 the dock company commissioned a paddlesteamer, the *Duchess of Devonshire*, to be joined by the *Duke of Devonshire* in 1894. The former was stranded on Sidmouth beach in 1934 and broken up where she lay. The latter was employed as a minesweeper in the Dardanelles during World War I, but returned to Exmouth as a pleasure steamer until her sale in 1932 to a Weymouth company, who renamed her *Consul*. She ended her sea-going days in 1965 when moved to the River Dart as an accommodation ship for a sailing club. After the First World War the docks continued to gain trade at the expense of their rivals upstream, and in 1934 and 1938 exceeded the tonnages discharged at Exeter, the principal cargoes, apart from coal and timber, being fertilisers, cider and potatoes. After the Second World War trade again revived, almost doubling in the decade before 1964, in which year some 200 vessels unloaded nearly 100,000 tons. More recent imports have included grains, animal foodstuffs, Esparto grass, woodpulp and starch. The persistent fears that Exmouth's trade would flourish at the expense of Exeter's have been amply justified.

The authorities have always considered it vital to control goods entering or leaving the mouth of the estuary. As early as 1364 three men were appointed to prevent the export of gold, silver and precious stones from Pratteshide, and there was a customs house at Exmouth by 1629. Despite the presence of the 'opposition', smugglers regularly plied their trade and in 1685 were landing contraband at Maer Brook and Watershott and in the isolated coves to the east. In that year two customs officers were reported for visiting a public house and, when the landlord promised to reward them, 'did not search but sate down and dranke for some time'. A new customs or watch house was built on the Point in about 1740, damaged by a storm in 1796 and destroyed by another in 1817. By the late 18th century a customs boat was regularly stationed at the river's mouth; its task was to surprise small boats slipping in from France. In December 1784 the *Alarm* lugger seized nearly 1,200 casks of spirits, a figure which gives some indication of the volume of traffic which must have gone undetected.

One gets the impression that 'everyone' was in the know, with a raft drifting in to shore bearing 130 barrels in 1791 and even the looker-out for wrecks himself trying to smuggle several ten-gallon casks that same year. In 1822 the aptly-named HM cutter *Scourge* brought in barrels thrown overboard by a smuggler's boat during a chase, and in 1827 a man caught signalling to a vessel from Maer Rocks with a lantern was rescued from the revenue officer before he could be locked up. The most embarrassing occasions came in 1831, when 50 gallons of brandy were found buried under the customs house, secreted by the officers themselves, and in 1856, when a coastguard cut his throat with a razor because he had failed to discover a contraband cargo. Much of the activity took place in the area of the Fairway buoy, a favourite marker for sinking weighted goods to be picked up later when the coast was clear. Many of the vessels and men arrested at Exmouth were from Beer, which appears to have been the major smuggling centre in the area. To the customs house were added the preventive houses, built by 1824 near the later lifeboat station. Subsequently used as the coastguard cottages, they were demolished in recent years to build a boating lake.

There is little early evidence of shipbuilding at Exmouth. In 1793 John Connett built the *Dolphin* privateer at the Point and Robert Connett a 47 ft cutter. In 1794 another cutter, the *Friends Goodwill*, was built by the Connetts, and in 1805 a Mr Davey launched the cutter *Surinam*. Matthew Lee Yeates and William Good, proprietors of the Exmouth Bank, leased nine acres of the Point in 1810 to build a repairing dock on the southern shore and a building yard on the northern. Unfortunately the bank failed in 1812 and, after constructing a warehouse and coalyard, they were forced to sell up. Both John Hayman and George Hooke were in business by 1824, the latter winning many cups in subsequent regattas. Another partnership, that of John Walters and James Wishart, had taken over the Point boatyard by 1828 and their launch of a 170 ton brig called the *Exmouth* attracted a crowd of 3,000 in 1839. Subsequently Walters went in for ropemaking at a ropewalk constructed nearby; in 1856 he built a new slip for the repair of vessels and in 1858 launched one of his largest ships, the schooner *Carmel*. However, the industry must be put into perspective. Only 11 Exmouth-built vessels were registered at Exeter during the years 1830-60, and of the 37 boats later built and owned by the Redways, probably only 14 were constructed at Exmouth. Larger tonnages could not be accommodated at the Point and a ship like their 550 ton *Magna Bona* had to be built at Teignmouth in 1856.

The Redway brothers, Thomas and Richard, started their business by acquiring the Point ropewalk about 1843, and in the 1860s employed many craftsmen in rope, sail, block and spar making, eventually adding shipbuilding to their repertoire. Thomas Dixon had established himself as a boatbuilder on the beach by 1848 and the Dixon family maintained the longest tradition of that craft in the town. But Exmothians never constructed iron vessels and lacking that expertise, the industry could only decline. When the Redways moved their yard to Dartmouth in 1869 it marked the end of shipbuilding on any substantial scale.

The ownership of wreckage washed up on the shore was claimed by the Earls of Devon as lords of the hundred. By the reign of Elizabeth I a court of the port or water of Exmouth was held before the Courtenays' water bailiff, at which all such wreckage had to be declared. The names of many features along the beach, their sites long forgotten, are preserved in these 16th century court records; a boat was found at Sallarmans Barn on the Meyre (Maer), a ship's pump picked up by Robert Gapper at Mary's Well next to the Meyre, a pair of oars valued at 10d washed up to the east of Red Rocke towards Offcumbe (Orcombe?) Clyffe, another oar found next to St Andrew's Pool in Littleham. Hundreds of early wrecks must have gone unrecorded or even unremarked. Early sailors had a healthy respect for the dangers of the Bar and the rocky ledges within it, but they regularly managed to fall foul of them. In 1764 the *Thomas Reed,* making from Plymouth to Guernsey, was blown off course and wrecked on the Bar, and in 1783 the collier *Francis and Hannah Dylers* went to pieces on the rocks. A year later the *Charles* from Rye, laden with wool, went aground on the Bar, although the crew was saved. Crews of ships stranded on the Bar were often rescued by staying with their vessels, but those that struck Maer Rocks or the Chickstone Ledge proved less fortunate. Despite the hazards, there were occasions when ships were saved. In 1794 the *Deborah Hooper,* coming in without a pilot, ran onto Maer Rocks but was successfully unladen and floated off. Perennial casualties were the stone boats that served the Maer lime kilns with limestone and culm from the early 18th century. They were obliged to come close inshore at high tide to throw the limestone overboard so that it could be collected from the beach at low water. A severe storm in July 1802 resulted in the sinking of one such stone boat on the Bar and the loss of two fishing boats and three lives. It was probably these losses which led to a public subscription for a lifeboat, and the fund had realised over £140 by December 1802. The vessel, 'a curious boat', arrived the following September, the cost largely defrayed by Lord Rolle, but there is no record of its use. In the years that followed, most of the successful rescues were made by pilots, as in 1807 when the *Fox* mistook Exmouth for Bridport. In 1812, when the *Brothers* of Poole ran onto the Pole Sands, the crew was rescued after spending the whole night in the rigging. A less creditable episode occurred in 1830, when a gang tried to plunder the wreck of the French *Marie.* In an October storm of 1836 the coastguards were the heroes, but two months later a hurricane sank both ferry boats, wrecked two trading vessels, blew the pilot sloops out to sea and wreaked havoc on the fishing fleet. A French vessel was lost with all hands in 1843 and another ship shared the same fate in 1851.

The entire cost of a second lifeboat with boat house was met by Lady Rolle in 1858 and the 30ft *Victoria* arrived the following year. The boat was first called out in 1866, but a year later an abortive attempt to rescue the *Julia* from the Pole Sands, when six lives were lost, led to some local criticism of both crew and boat. A new and larger lifeboat was acquired, again named *Victoria* and paid for by Lady Rolle, and a succession of vessels and lives have since been saved from this station. A further eight boats have followed the second *Victoria.* In 1878 the lifeboat on its carriage was towed by horses through country lanes to be launched at Budleigh Salterton. Although her crew was saved, it was the *Tehwija* which became one of the town's most spectacular wrecks at Orcombe in 1907. The saddest launch was on Christmas Day 1956, when two of the lifeboat crew were washed overboard and one,

William Carder, was drowned. From 1962 a larger lifeboat was kept afloat in the estuary and the boathouse, rebuilt in 1903, has since been used as a lifeboat museum. An inflatable inshore rescue boat was added to the station in 1966.

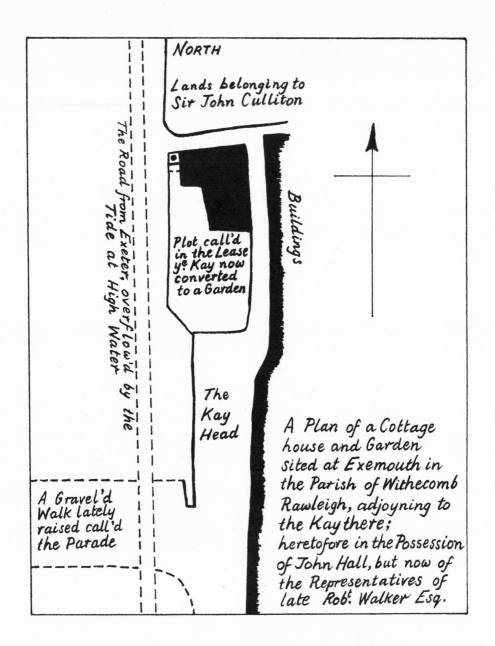

The origin of Exmouth: Pratteshide Quay, disused in 1759. Now the site of public conveniences in front of Glenorchy Church. Note the Parade, lately raised, and Exeter Road, inundated at high water. (ECM)

LEFT: Exmouth ferry station on the Point, by W. M. Craig, 1806. (EL)
RIGHT: Exmouth's coat of arms, granted 12 February 1947. (EL)
BELOW: Ferry Cottage on the Point, 1829. (EL)

30

The departure point for the Exmouth ferry at Starcross, 1822, (EL) and
BELOW: Passage House on the Point, by Emily H. Gould, 1835. (EL)

LEFT: Ferryman John arrives at the Warren, *c*1890. (LHNB) RIGHT: The first steam ferry, *Prince, c*1900. (LHNB) BELOW: Exmouth ferry before the Second World War. (LHNB)

32

LEFT: Sailing ship in Exmouth Docks, 1912. (LHNB) RIGHT: Exmouth cockle woman wields her rake. (LHNB) BELOW: The first visit of Exmouth pilot boat to Exeter Customs House, 1955. (EL)

ABOVE: Jetty at the Point in 1867 while the docks were being built. (EL)
BELOW: The dock offices and Mamhead View c1890. (LHNB)

34

ABOVE: Paddlesteamers in the Dock: *Duke* and *Duchess of Devonshire,*
and *King Edward, c*1910. (LHNB) CENTRE: *The Duke of Devonshire*
cutting a wake past Exmouth beach, 1905, (LHNB) and BELOW: the crew
of *The Duchess of Devonshire.* (LHNB)

ABOVE: Demolishing the former slipway at the Docks, 1932. (LHNB)
CENTRE: Club house of the Exmouth Yacht Club at the dock after the
fire of 26 February 1960. (EL) BELOW: Exmouth Dock in the 1950s.
(LHNB)

ABOVE: Aerial view of the docks. (LHNB) BELOW: 'Down your way'
comes to Exmouth: Bill Peters (left), dock master, interviewed by Richard
Dimbleby, 11 December 1949. (LHNB)

ABOVE: View from Teneriffe Walk, showing the preventive houses, 1860.
(EL) CENTRE: An early photograph of the coastguard station. (EL)
BELOW: Redway and Carter's yard on the Point. (EL)

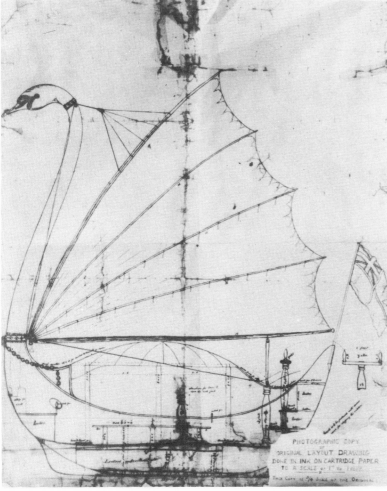

ABOVE: The barque *Memento* under construction in Redway's yard, 1869. (EL) BELOW LEFT: *The Swan of the Exe*, built for Capt G. Peacock of Starcross by Dixon and Son of Exmouth in 1860 at a cost of £130 15s 9¾d. (EL) RIGHT: The cabin of *The Swan:* fishing in comfort. (EL)

Launch of the Exmouth
a, 1859. (EL) CENTRE:
tion (right) and Harbour
NB) and BELOW: a new
and Mary Strachan, put
1960. (EL) CENTRE
rwegian brigantine, *John*
und on the Pole Sands,
TRE: The Sailors' Rest, St
, built 1908, now the
e Bureau and Further
tre. (LHNB) BELOW:
ng ship visiting Exmouth,
. (EL) RIGHT ABOVE:
he *Tehwija* at Orcombe
) BELOW: Shooting gulls
rly 19th century. (LHNB)

41

ABOVE: The Beacon from the Warren, 1829, (EL) and CENTRE:
Exmouth from the Warren, *c*1845. (EL) BELOW: A view of Exmouth from
the sea, 1882. (EL)

Resort of Repute

Exmouth has one great advantage over many other resort towns in looking out not over a blank expanse of sea, but on a broad stretch of coastal scenery beyond Torquay to Berry Head. To 18th century visitors the main attractions of the view were the twin parks of Mamhead and Powderham, which drew the eye across the estuary. In addition to these blessings, the western aspect of the town commands views of glorious sunsets which have inspired artists like Francis Danby, who lived for several years at Shell House on the Maer.

The traditional origin of Exmouth as a watering place was recorded in 1791 by Richard Polwhele, who said that the town was, 'little more than a century ago, only a small hamlet inhabited by fishermen. It was then brought into repute by one of the Judges of the circuit, who retired hither to bathe when in a very infirm state of health, and received great benefit'. It has never proved possible to identify this legal gentleman, but his recommendation was reinforced by the arrival of Sir John Colleton, a widely-travelled baronet and owner of Hille or Rill manor. He not only rebuilt a chapel at Withycombe, but raised a 'gravelled walk' called the Parade or sometimes 'the Terrace Walk', a sheltered promenade which once looked north across the estuary towards Powderham and Exeter.

The earliest evidence for sea bathing was noted at Whitby in 1718 and the first known bathing machine was recorded at Scarborough in 1735. This was the very period when the rich merchants and gentry of Exeter began to flock to Exmouth. According to Dr Pocock in 1750, the place was inhabited chiefly by fishermen and publicans ministering to these first day-trippers who came for 'diversion and bathing in the sea'. He went on: 'some people of condition have come to live at the place, which they are improving by a gravel walk to the river that is to be planted, and they are going to make a bowling green'. By 1755 'a neighbouring gentleman' had cut out of the rocks a primitive swimming bath, and by 1759 this was in regular use as being both safe and private. As far as we know, this was the earliest such bath in Devonshire, although its site cannot be traced. By 1760 George Zorn was staging concerts at Colleton's former house and advertising 'the famous tulip tree, now in blossom' as an added attraction. This was the *Magnolia Grandiflora Exmouthiensis*, introduced to England by Colleton, which now has its place on the town's crest. By 1765 the village's reputation had spread far beyond Exeter; in the words of one newspaper correspondent, it had become 'the Bath of the West, the resort of the tip-top of the gentry of the kingdom', already with two assembly rooms. By July of that year, lodgings were difficult to find and families were obliged to suffer 'the inconvenience of an inn' while waiting for accommodation to fall vacant.

The locals were quick to take advantage of their good fortune. By 1768, a coach service, the *Exmouth Machine,* was running regularly at 8.00am from Southernhay in Exeter at 2s 6d a seat, and two years later a new and larger vehicle was provided. In 1770 Robert Wood built a new assembly room and bowling green on the eastern edge of the Strand at the

Globe Inn, a public house first recorded about 1740. Wood held a public breakfast every Thursday and a card assembly on Mondays. There the Sieur Rea, a famous conjuror who used a swarm of live bees, performed in 1772. Sarah Morris's Exeter Inn, not to be outdone, boasted a fresh assortment of the best wines, a neat post chaise, able horses and careful drivers. The first regatta was held on the river in 1775, when a race to Teignmouth was won by an Exmouth boat, and a year later the Globe advertised a weekly subscription ball throughout the season at 2s 6d a time — including tea. As these balls were advertised in September, it indicates that the winter rather than the summer season was already becoming popular. News of a successful naval battle in 1780 was celebrated by the gentry on the Parade with an eleven-gun salute from the *Star* yacht and a procession to Chapel Hill.

On the beach the bathing machine was king. The early days of mixed and unclothed bathing and the boom in the sale of telescopes were long gone. The machines at Exmouth, which feature in many early engravings, were worked backwards and forwards by a windlass and not by horses as elsewhere. They were even the subject of an ode published in the *Gentleman's Magazine* in 1783. However, the harridans who kept the machines and acted as 'dippers' acquired a different reputation. Their mission in life was to ensure that their clients, no matter how unwilling, were fully immersed. One bewildered visitor described 'a form attired in coarse trousers with something on its head like a cowl', asked 'is the female form adapted to pantaloons?', and concluded 'by Jove, sir, it's too strong for Exmouth!' He was sadly in error. The dippers were to rule the beaches for over a century.

Despite its undoubted popularity, Exmouth remained largely uncommercialised; indeed, it was its rustic and picturesque appearance which had attracted its devotees in the first place. In 1782 it could still be described as a village 'composed of cot-houses, neat and clean, consisting of four or five rooms, which are generally let at a guinea a week'. There were no public buildings and the jaundiced eye of one observer found it all rather boring: 'no *belles dames* amusing to the unmarried but some *beldames* unamusing to the married'. He spent the days walking on the Beacon Hill, bathing and paying a visit or two, and the evening playing shilling whist or twopenny quadrille and tea-drinking. Others in that year lauded the 80-strong assemblies at the Globe, and later, the concerts held there from 1785. The place was a rural retreat, a settlement whose two-mile stretch of sand and dunes, uninterrupted by buildings and accessible only by footpaths, appealed to the romantics of an age which thought of itself as enlightened. Its days were numbered.

In 1790 an elegant new square was created on the Strand and walks laid out, probably below the Beacon. But of greatest significance was the granting of building leases on the Beacon Fields. On 11 April 1791 the first stone of the terrace was laid by the builder, John Staples, and the British flag was displayed. A cannon was fired, three 'huzzas' given, and the true British workmen retired to spend a guinea on drinking success to the building. The first two houses were completed before the year was out and gradually a long terrace arose, looking out over the panorama which had first drawn the wealthy to this spot. The Beacon houses were the first of many — not all, perhaps, as grand or as well-sited as those first homes, but they were to transform this village which was fast becoming a town. For the first time, people of quality could take lodgings befitting their station where, with their servants, they might while away the season in comfort.

Many visitors to Exmouth were not purely pleasure bent. They came to recover health — they came, literally, to a watering place. As long ago as 1754, Dr Richard Russell had announced that sea-bathing was actually harmful unless the bather drank a little over a quart of sea-water by way of 'hardening'. In 1791 one man thus toasted mine host of the Globe in sea-water:

'Hail, hospitable Wood, to thee I owe
Whate'er of Exmouth's beauteous scenes I know,
In this salubrious draught thy health I wish,
May'st thou in life ne'er want health, cash, nor fish.'

George III's physician, Dr Jebb, proclaimed that he rated the pureness of Exmouth's air above that of the South of France. When public baths opened here in 1800, it was thought natural that they should be run by a surgeon, Dr Glass Black, who five years later built a new marble bath for warm or cold sea-water bathing. Another successful bath was that opened in 1801 in Wellington Place, near the Globe, by Dr John Land, an expert in the treatment of scrofula, and a third had been constructed by Mr Maypee before 1825, when an unfortunate London customer expired on the premises. It is uncertain whether any of these were housed below the Beacon at the Bath House (now the Deer Leap public house) which was occupied as sea-water baths by Thomas Burridge in 1842 and continued as such for many years.

As the quality of life improved, so did that of the visitors. One of the growing town's greatest benefactors was the Emperor Napoleon, whose conflict in Europe closed France and the Grand Tour to the pleasure-loving English, forcing them to seek solace nearer home. By 1794 the Earl of Abergavenny had lighted on Exmouth for the winter season and his band played daily in the new square. Indeed, it was the presence of coastal military encampments during the wars that gave birth to the permanent association between brass bands and the seaside. After the military had departed, the town formed its own band in 1833, which used to play regularly on the Beacon. In 1795 a theatre was open three nights a week, possibly the one later noted on the Parade, and there were fortnightly balls at the Globe. Exmothians could marvel at the marriage of a local clergyman to a sister of the Earl of Erroll in 1797, the christening of a son of Lord Teignmouth in 1801 and the wedding of the Earl of Ormond in 1805. Yacht racing on the Exe was revived in 1801 and Joseph Ewen, a local builder, opened his new assembly rooms at the lower end of the Beacon in 1802. The most notorious resident at this time was Mary Ann Clarke, former actress and mistress of the Duke of York, who later published *and* was damned. She lived at Manchester House, in many ways a sad figure, her days of patronage and influence only a memory.

The war with France produced soaring inflation and by 1809 family lodgings on the Beacon fetched between three and seven guineas a week. Fortunately, such prices did not even dent the town's popularity. It was the era of the circulating library, a centre not merely for the borrowing of books, but where ladies might view the latest fashions on others and, of more importance, be admired wearing them themselves. Miss Langsford's library appeared first in 1809, then Miss Ewen's in 1811 and later others. Strange that the town had to wait until 1946 for its public library. The regattas in the estuary became an annual occasion; by 1819 they included pony and donkey racing, wrestling and 'jumping in sacks', and by 1835, rowing races for women. In 1841 the Exmouth band played afloat, 'their dulcet strains deriving increased sweetness in the reverberations from the water'. By 1855 the regatta had been combined with an archery fête, when a triumphal arch was set up in the town, bearing the initials of Victoria and Albert and of Napoleon III and Eugenie. The French were receiving their due at last. In 1863 the celebrations included the novel contest of walking the greased bowsprit of a ship anchored in the Bight. The prize, a pig in a box, was suspended at the end of the spar.

45

Other attractions mounted in the town included a two-day wrestling match in 1827 which attracted Abraham Cann, the champion of England; another was held behind the London Inn in 1829. Exmothians were introduced to the latest dance, the *Gallopade en quadrille,* at a Christmas ball at the Globe in 1830. In 1842 Van Amburgh's circus elephant caused a sensation by bathing in the sea, and in 1846 the celebrated General Tom Thumb came to the town. On a higher plane, the Rev Francis Bishop drew large crowds to the Albion Rooms for a lecture in 1848, although the authorities took a dim view of skittle-playing at the Dolphin until 12.30 at night in 1859.

It was the same era that brought the two best-remembered visitors to the town. Lady Nelson was in residence by 1820, when her grandson was born here; she threw a grand ball and supper for her new-found acquaintances at the London Inn in 1821, and in 1829 moved into a house in Louisa Place. After her death in London in 1831, she joined other members of her family in a vault in Littleham churchyard. Lady Byron and her daughter spent the autumn of 1828 at Chapman's Beacon Hotel, now no. 19. Other illustrious guests included the Grand Duchess Helene in 1831, the exotic Mariana Starke, the 'Queen of Sorrento', who presented her 'Tableaux Vivants' at a ball at Ewen's Rooms in 1832, and Franz Liszt, who performed at the Beacon Hotel, now the Manor Hotel, in 1840.

Such visitors demanded improved facilities. There was a new drive along the beach by 1824, ornamented from that year with William Kendall's idealised temples. The journey from London to Exmouth by sea broke the three-day barrier in 1827, a new theatre was 'fitted up' near the London Inn in 1829 and the walks on the Beacon, begun in 1828, were railed in 1834. From 1840 the steam yacht *Alert* plied between Exeter and Exmouth twice a day at 1s a trip, until it was impounded to pay the crew's wages. Accompanied by a salute of 19 guns, the foundation stone of the two-mile sea wall was laid in 1841, paid for, yet again, by Lord Rolle; the wall was completed the next year. It alone facilitated the development of the sea front.

But as the years passed, so did Exmouth's zenith as a watering place, and the reason is not hard to find. While the expanding towns of Dawlish, Teignmouth and, above all, Torquay were linked to a growing national railway network, the traveller to Exmouth still had to board his horse-drawn carriage at Exeter and jolt his way to the sea. A railway to the town had been suggested as early as 1825, but it was killed by the fear that it would cripple Exeter's trade, a fear shared by the noble Lord Rolle with his substantial investment in the Exeter Canal. Another scheme floated in 1845 met a similar fate, and it was not until 1858 that the first sod was cut by John Walter of Marpool — and even then his spade broke. The start of operations was delayed and it was May Day 1861 when the first train steamed into the town. Triumphal arches bespattered the streets, bearing slogans such as 'Excursions for the Million', 'Increase of our Trade', 'Success to the Iron Road', 'May all our Hopes be realised' and, more to the point, 'Time is Money'. In the first five days 10,000 people travelled on the line and property values increased overnight. By the 1880s commuter traffic into Exeter was considerable, and a double track was installed beyond Topsham by the First World War. The station at Exmouth was rebuilt in 1926, and by 1957 the number of tickets collected at Exmouth was almost as high as those taken at Exeter Central. The link to Budleigh Salterton, with a station at Littleham, was opened in 1903, but fell a victim to rail cuts in 1967.

Soon after the arrival of the railway, the centre of Exmouth was transformed. The east of the old village had been a rabbit warren of thatched cottages, but a succession of fires had destroyed a number of them and in 1863 Lord Rolle laid out a new street, which obliterated many of the old courts and tenements that remained. The first shop in Rolle Street was built in 1868 and the whole was completed about 1875. From that time the modern resort and town began to take shape. The Strand Gardens were secured by the town in 1870 and the Manor Grounds, leased in 1893, were opened three years later and given by the Rolles in 1907. The Manor House on Chapel Hill came down in 1894, and the gardens there were enlarged in 1905. On the sea front, the Clock Tower was set up for Victoria's Jubilee in 1897 and the Queen's Drive constructed to continue the esplanade eastwards. The Beach Gardens were laid out in 1904, the Marine Drive to Orcombe was completed in 1920 and the Pavilion in 1933. The only blot on this continuous and continuing expansion was and is the litter of beach huts along so much of the sea front — formerly on the beach itself, they were moved after the last war to the inshore side of the road.

Centres of public entertainment have included Thorn's Commercial Coffee Palace, where popular concerts were given in the late 19th century, and the Public Hall, now the Savoy Cinema, opened on the Strand in 1887, where the first moving pictures were seen. The Pier pavilion, established in 1894, later included a skating rink. 'Talkies' were first shown in 1930 at the King's Kinema, later renamed the Grand and now the Royal, although the Forum Cinema has since succumbed to Bingo. The former Manor Hall beside the Manor Grounds has had a chequered career as the Regal Cinema, ballroom, bowling alley and nightclub.

Organised sport was a relatively late addition to the town's attractions. The first recorded cricket match was played in 1843 between Exmouth and Sidmouth, when the latter won by 48 runs, and the afternoon was 'enlivened' by the playing of a foreign band. A cricket club had been founded by 1851, holding a dinner to celebrate the opening of the season at the Beacon Assembly Rooms, but had lapsed within three years. The present club was founded in 1860 and a pavilion built in 1867. The archery club started in 1855 after the contest held that year in conjunction with the regatta. The sport was particularly popular with the ladies, who competed from the beginning. There were 73 entrants at the annual meeting of 1858 and a toxophilite ball was a feature of that season. Under the archery club's wing there gathered croquet, tennis by 1881 and from 1894 bowls. The Madeira Bowling Club was formed in 1926 and when the tennis club lost its courts to the Council in 1922, it found a new home at Cranford.

A swimming club, using the dock, was in being by 1885 and a swimming pool was started, but never completed, by Camperdown Terrace in 1889. The Exmouth Swimming and Life Saving Society, founded in 1893, instituted the Long Swim from Starcross. Since the building of the swimming pool below Gun Cliff in 1932, the weekly galas (in which the author competed) have provided regular summer entertainment. The golf club commenced its activities in 1886 and the remains of the bunkers can still be traced on the Maer. The rugby club, now resited on the Imperial recreation ground, was formed in 1888, there were two football clubs by 1892, and a cycling club started in 1907. For those who preferred more leisurely activities, the Exmouth Club, now the aquarium, was built on the sea front in 1889. Many other societies have flourished in the town and tribute should perhaps be paid to the operatic society, founded in 1910, and the Exmouth Players, both of which have managed to raise smiles on the faces of the dourest Exmothians.

Exmouth's two miles of sand have determined the character of the 20th century resort. It is still relatively unspoilt, and over the years has become a mecca for yachtsmen, anglers, and particularly for families — the happy site of a million and one transitory sandcastles.

ABOVE: View of Exmouth from Powderham Castle, 1850. (LHNB)
BELOW: Exmouth sea wall, 1860.

ABOVE: Teneriffe (now Madeira) Walk, 1871, showing 'Miramar' (left), cricket ground (centre) and lime kiln in the distance. (EL) CENTRE: The Estuary from Gun Cliff, 1860. BELOW: Beneath the Beacon, 1871, showing the Bath House — now the Deer Leap. (EL)

ABOVE: Globe Hotel, the former centre of Exmouth's night life, demolished *c*1866 to build Rolle Street. Entrance to Market Street is on the left. (EL) BELOW LEFT: Lord Teignmouth was an early visitor in 1800. (MC) RIGHT: Mary Anne Clarke, 1810: Exmouth's most notorious 'lady'. (MC)

Mary Anne Clarke soliciting favours from the Duke of York. (MC)

51

INSET: While the 'ladies' played, the players worked: Edmund Kean (here as Shylock) appeared at Exmouth Theatre c1810. (MC) ABOVE: A barren shore: the view below Beacon Hill looking towards Lobster Hall and Manchester Quay, 1806. (EL) BELOW: A romanticised view of the Beacon and Point windmill, c1830. (EL)

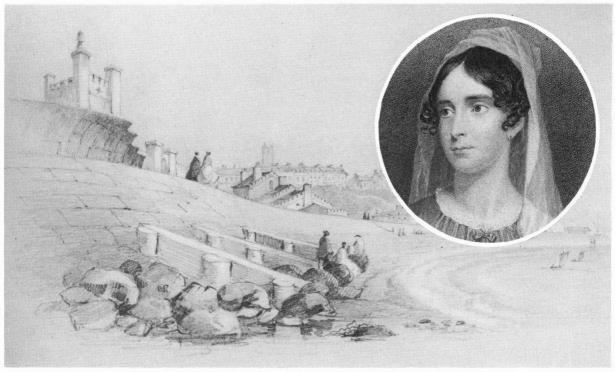

ABOVE LEFT: Bastin's Royal Beacon Hotel, 1872, moved from the present Manor Hotel *c*1860. RIGHT: The widow of Trafalgar, Lady Nelson, pictured in 1804. She lived in the town and was buried at Littleham 1831. (MC) INSET BELOW: Lady Byron, a visitor to Chapman's Beacon Hotel, in 1828. (MC) BELOW: The sea wall soon after its completion, *c*1845. (EL)

ABOVE: The Point from the Beacon Walks, c1845, (EL) and BELOW: An 1870 photograph of the Point, showing, in the distance, Beach Castle and in the foreground, the Temple of Theseus. (LHNB)

54

ABOVE: The Temple below the Beacon, c1830. (LHNB) CENTRE: The crowded estuary seen from the Beacon, c1845. (EL) BELOW: Trefusis Terrace, c1870, with the new cricket pavilion on the extreme right. (LHBN)

LEFT ABOVE: *Sketch o*
approaches her clients. (W
*c*1845, which brought the
Reading at the Assembly
Commercial Temperance
known as the Coffee Pal
BELOW: John England's
Cha

at Exmouth; a dreaded 'dipper'
W: New Road (later Carlton Hill)
o the town. (EL) CENTRE: Penny
. (EL) RIGHT ABOVE: Thorn's
Station Parade, the hall of which,
me the Forum Cinema. (LHNB)
's shop, the former Exeter Inn, in
90. (LHNB)

LEFT ABOVE: Sprague's Beach Hotel, burnt down c1895. (LHNB) BELOW: The Iron Horse arrives in Exmouth, 1861. (EL)

RIGHT ABOVE: A grand procession to mark the belated Exeter Connection, (EL) and BELOW: When, where and how to get to and from Exmouth in 1865.

PROGRAMME OF THE

PROCESSION

FOR CELEBRATING THE OPENING OF

The Exeter & Exmouth Railway

ON THE 1st OF MAY, 1861.

The Procession will meet the Exeter and Exmouth Directors at the Terminus.

Police Constables.
ARTILLERY BAND.
VOLUNTEER ARTILLERY.
VOLUNTEER RIFLES.
COAST-GUARD & NAVAL RESERVE.
THE ROYAL STANDARD.
GENERAL COMMITTEE.
FLAGS, &c.
EXMOUTH BRASS BAND.
DIRECTORS OF THE RAILWAY.
FLAGS.
TRADESMEN, &c.
THE EXMOUTH CLUBS.
NATIONAL AND OTHER SCHOOLS.
Littleham National School.
Withycombe ditto.
Glenorchy Sunday School.
Ebenezer ditto.
Wesleyan Methodist ditto.
Brethren's ditto.
Primitive Methodist ditto.
Ragged School.

The Procession will be formed at 12.30 p.m., and proceed, punctually at 1 o'clock, by the following

ROUTE:

On the Parade and Exeter-road, up North-street, across Brunswick Terrace, down Albion-street, under the Parade, on the Strand, to the Beacon and Terraces, turn at Teneriffe House into the New-road by Mrs. Acton's, and proceed by Louisa Terrace, the Beacon, and Temple Road, through Mr. Webber's Field, to the Rope-walk Field.

The Artillery and other Companies should be formed on the Parade. The School Children will muster in the Square opposite Mr. Mansfield's house. Each Master will carry a Number, and take the Children under his care to the Field, and to the Table bearing the Number corresponding to the one he carries. Immediately on the return of the Procession to the Strand, the Testimonial will be presented to J. H. Walker Aylesbury, Esq.

The Public Dinner at the Globe Hotel will take place at 3 o'clock.

IT IS REQESTED THAT ALL BUSINESS BE SUSPENDED.

TIME TABLE.—EXETER AND EXMOUTH RAILWAY.
Corrected for FEBRUARY, 1865.

UP.	Week Days.							Sundays.				
	1, 2, 3 a.m.	1, 2, 3 a.m.	1, 2, 3 p.m.	1, 2, 3 p.m.	1, 2, 3 p.m.	1, 2, 3 p.m.	1, 2, 3 p.m.	1, 2, 3 p.m.	1, 2, 3 p.m.	1, 2, 3 p.m.	1, 2, 3 p.m.	1, 2, 3 p.m.
EXMOUTH ..	6 50	9 0	12 30	2 20	4 -	7 0	9 0	9 45	1 0	5 15	7 45	..
Lympstone.. ..	6 56	9 6	12 36	2 26	4 35	7 6	9 6	9 51	1 6	5 21	7 51	..
Woodbury Road	7 1	9 11	12 41	2 31	4 39	7 11	9 11	9 56	1 11	5 26	7 56	..
Topsham ..	7 6	9 16	12 46	2 36	4 45	7 16	9 16	10 1	1 16	5 31	8 1	..
EXETER	7 18	9 30	1 0	2 50	4 55	7 28	9 28	10 15	1 30	5 45	8 15	..

DOWN.	Week Days.							Sundays.				
	1, 2, 3 a.m.	1, 2, 3 a.m.	1, 2, 3 p.m.	1, 2, 3 p.m.	1, 2, 3 p.m	1, 2, 3 p.m.	1, 2, 3 p.m.	1, 2, 3 a.m.	1, 2, 3 a.m.	1, 2, 3 p.m.	1, 2, 3 p.m.	1, 2, 3 p.m.
EXETER	8 0	10 15	1 15	3 50	6 10	7 45	9 50	..	10 30	2 30	6 10	8 30
Topsham	8 14	10 29	1 29	4 4	6 24	7 59	10 4	..	10 44	2 44	6 24	8 44
Woodbury Road	8 19	10 34	1 34	4 9	6 29	8 4	10 9	..	10 49	2 49	6 29	8 48
Lympstone ..	8 24	10 39	1 39	4 14	6 34	8 9	10 14	..	10 54	2 54	6 34	8 54
EXMOUTH	8 30	10 45	1 45	4 20	6 40	8 15	10 20	..	11 0	3 0	6 40	9 0

ABOVE: The station on Opening Day, 1861. (LHNB) BELOW: Bastin's coach leaves the Station, probably carrying guests for the Royal Beacon Hotel, c1870. (EL)

ABOVE: The Great Tree outside the station marked the parish boundary between Littleham and Withycombe, c1865. (LHNB) BELOW: The railway station before demolition in 1926. (LHNB)

ABOVE: The second station, *sans* clock, 1974, (LHNB) and BELOW: the not-so-permanent way between platforms, also in 1974. (LHNB)

ABOVE: Out for a stroll along the Prom, *c*1910. (EL) BELOW: Time to sit, stare, paddle or chat. Summer bungalows, Pier, Pavilion, pleasure boat — and working sail at Shelley Beach, *c*1912. (EL)

LEFT: Exmouth's answer to Victoria's Jubilee: the Clock Tower, 1897.
(LHNB) ABOVE RIGHT: The Pier Pavilion c1920, (EL) and BELOW:
Sporting confusion at the Regatta off Temple Steps. (LHNB)

64

ABOVE: The Esplanade, earlier this century. (LHNB) BELOW: The
Savoy Cinema, formerly the Public Hall, opened in 1887 on the Strand.
(LHNB)

ABOVE: The Imperial Hotel advertises; Morton Crescent and Gertrude Terrace have been carefully removed and a sylvan setting substituted. (LHNB) BELOW: Disaster at the Imperial. After the tragic fire of 1974. (LHNB)

66

ABOVE LEFT: The Exmouth Amateur Dramatic Society, 1926/7. (EL)
RIGHT: The last vestige of the Albert Hall in Margaret Street, demolished
1977. (LHNB) BELOW: Lady toxophilites showing their prowess on the
archery ground before Claremont Terrace *c*1870. (EL)

67

Local Time Tables to Sept. 29th, 1907.

LAUNCH TO STARCROSS.

Exmouth for Starcross.

*7, 7-35, 8-40, 10-30, 11-20 a.m.; 12-30, 1-15, 2-40, 3-50, 5-5, 5-50, 6-40, 7-30, 8-55 p.m.

SUNDAYS:—8-40, 9-35 a.m.; 1-25, 2-25, 6-30 p.m.

Starcross for Exmouth.

*7-40, 8-30, 9-20, 11-15 a.m.: 12-25, 1-10, 2-30, 3-30, 4-30, 5-30, 6-18, 7-5, 8-5, 9.30 p.m.

SUNDAYS:—9-15, 10-15 a.m.; 2, 3, 8.15 p.m.

*Mondays only.

EXMOUTH & EXETER BRANCH.

Exmouth for Exeter.

6-45, 7-58, 9, 9-30, 9-43, 11-25, 12-10, 1-25, 2-15, 3-30, 4-25, 5-20, 6-5, 7, 7-45, 8-35, 9-15, 10-40.

SUNDAYS:—9-15, 1-5, 2-50, 4-55, 8-10, 9.30.

Exeter for Exmouth.

6-45, 8, 9, 10-20, 11-25, 12-50, 1-25, 2-12, 2-55, 4-27, 5-20, 6-12, 6-30, 7, 7-47, 8-35, 10-10, 11.

SUNDAYS:—7-30, 10-20, 2-20, 4-20, 6, 8-55.

BUDLEIGH SALTERTON BRANCH.

Exmouth for Salterton.

6-40, 8-40, 10-51, 11-24, 12-10, 1-23, 2-50, 4-15, 4-58, 6-35, 7-36, 9-20.

SUNDAYS:—10-55, 2-55, 6-35.*

Salterton for Exmouth.

9-10, 11-6, 11-39, 1-5, 2-9, 3-58, 4-53, 5-46, 7-14, 7-53, 8-56, 9-40.

SUNDAYS:—12-45, 4-35, 7.50.

Season's Attractions.

ISSUE No. 5.

August 25th, at 3.15 p.m.—"Men's Own" at the Parade Church; Speaker, Mr. Worth, of Exeter.

On the Sands each day, Services for Children at 11 a.m., Adults at 8 p.m. Sundays, 3 and 8.

August 26th.—Cricket Match—Ealing Dean C.C. v. Exmouth.

August 26th.—200 yards Club Challenge Handicap Race at the Docks.

August 27th.—Cricket Match—Old Tauntonians.

August 28th.—A Grand Concert at the Manor Grounds arranged by the Exmouth Tradesmen's Association. By special request, return visit of the Band of the Royal Artillery (Plymouth Division). Bandmaster Evans. Evening at 8. Brilliant Illumination of the Grounds by thousands of Fairy Lights and Chinese Lanterns.

September 2nd.—"The Holiday of the Season"—Exmouth Athletic Sports, in the Cricket Field, at 1.30 p.m. Foot Races and Cycle Races. Entries include some of the well-known Champions of the day.

Grand Illuminated Concert in the Manor Grounds in the Evening. Band of the 4th Battalion Devonshire Regiment.

Each day on the Queen's Drive, High-class Concerts are given by the "Courtiers" Concert Party, at 3.15 and 8. Chairs, 2d. each.

Military Concerts at the Manor Grounds on September 4th and 11th.

Refreshments may be obtained at Andrews' Restaurant, Victoria-road, near Station and Pier; also at Thorn's Temperance Hotel (4 doors from Station), or at Thorn's Pleasure Grounds, near the Queen's Drive and Esplanade.

ABOVE: Exmouth sits down to luncheon, celebrating Edward VII's Coronation, 9 August 1902. (EL) BELOW: Riding high. Sellers Carriage Proprietors, Belgrave Place, Station Parade, 1910. (EL)

ABOVE: The Methodists take a charabanc outing from the Parade, c1920.
(LHNB) CENTRE: Exmouth United AFC, 1926/7, winners of the Peek
Senior Shield, the Passmore Junior Shield and the Orchard Cup. (EL)
BELOW: Exmouth still draws the crowds. At Orcombe Point in the sunny
seventies. (LHNB)

70

The Plantation below the Beacon then and now — *c*1910 and today.
(LHNB)

ABOVE: The old Market House (right) on the Strand, 1858, demolished 1869. (EL) BELOW: Sauntering on the Strand after the market had gone, 1871.

Millers and Merchants

Those who lived on the nearly 4,900 acres comprising the two ancient parishes must have survived principally on agriculture, and would have been largely self-sufficient. The soil was rich and the area heavily populated, even in the Middle Ages. Although there were small villages at Bradham, Littleham and at Exmouth itself, most of the land was divided between scattered farmsteads, probably by 1086, if they are represented by the 23 villeins or farmers recorded in Domesday Book. Many of these farms survive today; some, like Cranford, Brixington and Bapton, overtaken by the expanding town, others, like Quaintance, Liverton and Woodlands, still being worked. These settlements were served by a network of roads which paid scant regard to coastal access, and concentrated on linking farms and hamlets with each other and driving beyond — to East Budleigh, to the ridgeway running north across Woodbury Common and along the estuary to Topsham and Exeter.

Mediaeval Exmouth was served by what is now Exeter Road, which ran along the foreshore of the river by the 13th century and was still inundated at high water five hundred years later. It continued along the line of the later Chapel and High Streets to mount Chapel Hill. Traffic, if laden pack animals, horsemen and pedestrians can be called traffic, passed at high tide down Gypsy Lane, over Marpool Hill and down into Exmouth by way of North, Margaret, or Fore streets. There was no Rolle Street, no Albion Street. Exeter Road was not turnpiked until 1832, when toll gates were set up at Courtlands Cross and near the present library. The Budleigh road reached the town by means of Long Causeway, probably the causeway on which Littleham church wardens lavished large sums of money in 1657.

The Strand, as its name implies, was a sandy shore behind the shelter of the Point, around which a semicircle of houses had been built by the 17th century and probably much earlier. Some were large, such as Whitrow's and Wade's 'Great' houses, occupied principally by merchants and shipowners. Certain farmers, like Benedict Whitrow of Cranford, had both a house in the country and another in the town. Chapel Street was evidently built up by the 14th century, the area west towards the Strand and around the Cross, and Chapel Hill, by the 15th. Archaeological excavations in 1977 on the site of the new central development produced pottery dating from the late 13th century and evidence of 14th and 15th century buildings. Once these streets had been occupied, the less well-off — the fishermen, sailors and pilots — extended the settlement inland, particularly along South Street, to fill the shallow valley north of the present Rolle Street, an area formerly known as South Town. The redevelopment of this whole area in the 19th century almost completely obliterated the former shipping village 'withyn the haven mouth'. Land reclamation has totally distorted the western shoreline. It began with the building of the Parade in the first half of the 18th century, and was continued in 1811. In that year William

73

Thomas Hull of Marpool, as lord of Hille or Rill, built the embankment along which the railway approaches the station, enclosing over 50 acres, on which building started in 1895. Further reclamation by the station and in front of Imperial Road started in 1932, and from 1935 became the George V pleasure grounds.

The life of a prosperous merchant on the Strand was, as might be expected, dominated by the sea. In 1523, Widow Rede of Withycombe demanded a reduced tax assessment for a boat taken by the French, three men claimed relief for goods submerged by the sea and John Randall of Littleham wrote off £9 owed to him by the Earl of Wiltshire for fresh and salt fish, 'the whycche woll never be payde'. The buying and selling of agricultural produce, fish and imported commodities which the area could not supply for itself were vital to the economy of the growing town.

Both Exmouth and Littleham villages had mediaeval markets, the origins of which are unrecorded. References to a market place at Littleham occur in the 15th century, and in 1456 16 men were fined as 'common regrators' in Exmouth market: namely, people who bought goods when the market opened and resold them later at a higher price. A similar misdemeanour was committed by William Hoygge in 'the market of Chyxston' by buying and selling fish in 1500, and Thomas Cadyford 'forestalled' the market in 1560 by buying up goods before they reached the market place. The Exmouth market was at first held in that area of Market Street formerly known as the Cross, where in 1755 there was still a ruined cross around which the butchers plied their trade on Wednesdays and Saturdays. In 1539 Sir Thomas Dennys and the people of Exmouth were granted the right to hold two fairs there: on the eve and day of St Mark (24-25 April) and the eve and day of SS. Simon and Jude (27-28 October). The fairs were evidently run by Littleham churchwardens, who received 6s 8d from each. In 1630 they paid for timber to make 32 trestles, used as fair stalls, which were stored in the Church House at Littleham.

The two fairs were of 'small importance' by 1830, although by 1848 the markets had been increased to three days with the addition of Tuesdays. Lord Rolle built a new market house at the southern end of the Strand Enclosure in 1827, to replace an earlier one in Fore Street. The building was elegantly decorated when the town sat down there to celebrate young Mark Rolle's coming of age in 1856. A new market was completed in 1869 on the site of the present church hall, and replaced in about 1914 by a small pannier market and weighbridge in South Street. The fairs became occasions for pleasure rather than commerce long before they ceased in 1914.

Three of the manors in the Exmouth area had their own corn or grist mills. In about 1170 Walter de Claville granted Withycombe Mill to Canonsleigh Priory, together with six acres nearby. The grant included the requirement that all Withycombe manor tenants should grind their corn there. It was not mentioned thereafter but must have stood on the Withycombe Brook to the north-east of Bradham Lane. It was probably superseded by two mills in Bradham manor, mentioned in the 13th century. The tithes from them were granted to St Nicholas' Priory by the Prioress of Polsloe, in return for 2s a year paid to Withycombe church. These were probably the two mills leased with Marpool in 1557, as there was only one miller in Withycombe in the 16th century, regularly fined in the hundred court for demanding excessive tolls — as were most millers. The two mills evidently stood in the area of the later Marpool or Withycombe Mill. The miller, Ephraim Williams, went bankrupt in 1849 but declined to give up the mill until he had taken his apple crop from the orchard. The mill was stoned by a mob during the bread riots of 1867 and was only demolished in 1962 as part of the great flood-prevention scheme which

74

followed the floods of 1960. The wheel, however, was rescued and is preserved in the gardens below the Beacon.

Littleham had a windmill by 1388, which continued to grind until the 16th century, and probably stood either in fields called Windmill in the corner of West Down and Gore lanes, or near the junction of Sarlsdown and Salterton roads, where there was another field of the same name. A second windmill was built on the Point in 1797 by a Mr Champling, who was killed by a blow from one of its sails in 1799, 'leaving two orphan sons to lament the loss of a tender father'. In 1818 a gale carried the sails round so fast that the machinery caught fire and destroyed the upper part of the structure. It was disused by 1825, still standing in 1830, but probably demolished soon after.

One trade not linked with either sea or land was lacemaking, a cottage industry which had begun to dominate the female labour market by the mid-18th century. The manufacture had originally spread from Honiton and by 1818 there were no fewer than 26 lace schools attended by 393 children in the town. The vicar of Littleham, Richard Prat, complained of them as a great obstacle to girls' attendance at the National School and considered them to be 'more productive of evil than good, as they incapacitate the girls, when grown up, from attending to their domestic occupations'. The scale of the industry can be gauged from the fact that there were ten lace-making businesses in the town in 1848 and that in Fore Street alone there were 38 lace workers, women and children, in 1851. When Isaac Beer of Fore Street died in 1863, his stock of lace and lace sprigs was sufficiently large to be sold by tender. The earnings of many a fisherman's family were supplemented by the lace trade throughout the 19th and even into the 20th century.

The rapid growth of Exmouth from the second half of the 18th century took place at a time when most houses were built of brick. A thriving brick and tile business was established in Withycombe village in about 1775 by Robert Brice (died 1799) and carried on by his widow until her death in 1827. By 1831 the premises were held by John Daw, when he was accused of evading duty on his four months' production of 45,000 bricks. One of his successors, Henry Doble, was killed by a fall from a hayrick in 1857, leaving a widow and nine children unsupported. By 1858 the works were in the hands of Edward Carter, whose family built many houses in the town and established the brickworks on the Budleigh road towards the end of the century. Other brick kilns were in operation at Rill by 1860, remodelled by Thomas Redway in 1873, and also at Mudbank and in Watery Lane.

However, the general pattern of employment, as might be expected in a resort, was domestic service for the poor and shop and office work for others. Despite the influx of supermarkets and large stores, there are still businesses which, although their ownership may have changed, can trace their origins back well into the 19th century: businesses like Bickford's chemists or Clapp's cafe, formerly a bakery which was severely damaged in the bread riots of 1867. The keynote, as in most matters associated with 19th century Exmouth, was one of gradual expansion. There was a distressing number of bankruptcies in trade, but the number of milliners and dressmakers rose from one in 1824 to eighteen in 1848 and of hairdressers from none to four in the same period.

The largest inns, which served visitors to the town from the 18th century, were augmented by hotels established during the 19th. Some, such as those on the Beacon, were converted dwelling houses; others, like the Imperial in 1869, were purpose-built. In recent years the trend has been partly reversed and some hotels like the Maer Bay, converted from the 19th century mansion, Miramar, have turned into flats, or, like the Pencarwick, once a famous private school for boys, demolished to build more flats. Today the town is less fully committed to the resort image than in the past, and has become more of a residential and retirement centre. Although many occupations are still seasonal, for here the seaside landlady and her guest house will never die, the town does not sleep through the winter. There are far too many social and and vocational activities to be pursued. Rather, it heaves a small sigh as the beaches clear and shopping queues shorten; Exmothians who dislike crowds more than winter weather emerge, the esplanade defences against the shifting sands are raised and the cycle starts again.

Where the stone boats discharged: the 18th century lime kilns on the Maer.
(EL)

ABOVE: Green Farm, Maer Lane, Littleham, 1914. (LHNB) BELOW:
Marpool or Withycombe Mill, *c*1890, with members of the Long family,
millers. (EL)

ABOVE: The windmill on the Point, built in 1797 — the idyllic scene before the docks came. (LHNB) BELOW: An uneasy survivor: the windmill surrounded by resort development in 1829. (EL)

78

ABOVE: Town meets country at Humphries' smithy in Withycombe village, *c*1910. (LHNB) BELOW: Stocker's saddlery, demolished *c*1948, next to the Hollytree Inn, Withycombe; pictured in the late 19th century. (EL)

ABOVE: The waves wash the back of the Parade in 1805, six years before Hull's embankment reclaimed this area on which the 'Colony' now stands. (EL) BELOW: The parting of the ways — Fore Street meets Church Street c1900. (LHNB)

ABOVE: John Clode's bakery van pauses on Chapel Hill by Dodd's Dairy, near Mrs Ferris's crab shop *c*1910. (LHNB) BELOW: Thomas Abell made the bricks and built the houses for an expanding Exmouth. (LHNB)

ABOVE: The clever Miss Copp offered to share her craft as late as 1902,
(LHNB) and CENTRE: the confident Mrs Hutchings paraded her delicate
wares in 1872. BELOW: a prize-winning carthorse in Phear Park parade.
(LHNB)

82

EXMOUTH.

TO BE SOLD

BY AUCTION,

BY MR. THOMAS CRUDGE,

On THURSDAY the 24th day of MAY, 1866,

Precisely at Four o'clock in the Afternoon,

AT BAKER'S ALBION INN, EXMOUTH,

Subject to such Conditions as shall be there produced, the undermentioned

FREEHOLD

HOUSES,

VIZ:—

LOT 1. All that desirable Dwelling House and Premises, with Garden in Front, situate and being No. 3, Albion Terrace, Exmouth, now in the occupation of Mr. J. ADAMS.

LOT 2. All that Dwelling House adjoining, now in the occupation of Mr. SPLATT.

Each House comprises two Parlours, two best Bedrooms, Dressing Room, two Attics, Water Closet, Kitchen, Pantry, Housekeeper's Room, Court Yard, and all necessary domestic offices.

The Property may be Viewed by permission of the Tenants, and further information obtained of the AUCTIONEER, or of

Messrs. SANDERS & BURCH,

SOLICITORS AND PROCTORS, PALACE GATE, EXETER.

W. M. BOUNSALL, PRINTER, EXMOUTH.

Thomas Crudge offered two desirable residences in 1866.

83

EXMOUTH,
DEVON.

To be SOLD
BY AUCTION,

By Mr. S. DAY,

On THURSDAY, the 31st day of DECEMBER inst.,

At Two o'Clock in the Afternoon,

AT GIFFORD'S LONDON INN, IN EXMOUTH AFORESAID,

ALL THOSE THREE

DWELLING
HOUSES

WITH

THE OFFICES THERETO BELONGING,

AND

WORKSHOP ADJOINING,

SITUATE NEARLY OPPOSITE THE TURNPIKE GATE AT THE ENTRANCE TO THE TOWN OF EXMOUTH,

Now in the several Occupations of WILLIAM KNIGHT, FANNY LARMEY, JOHN LANGDON, MARY HAYNE, EDMUND EADES, and RICHARD HARRIS, as Tenants, and producing a Rental of £32 19s. per Annum.

These Premises are held under a Lease from the Mayor, Bailiffs, and Commonalty of Exeter, for a Term of 99 Years, which commenced 25th MARCH, 1830, determinable on the Death of the Survivor of 3 Lives, aged respectively 29, 30, and 31 Years, under the Yearly Conventionary Rent of £2.

The respective Tenants will shew the Premises; and further particulars may be obtained on application to Mrs. SOUTHCOTT, Exmouth; or

MESSRS. SANDERS & KITSON,
SOLICITORS, EXETER.

Dated 14th December, 1846.

R. J. Trewman, Printer, Exeter

The former ferry site on the route into town. Three houses on Mona Island come under the hammer in 1846.

Horsepower gives way to motor traction. ABOVE: The last horse-drawn mail coach leaves town, 31 May 1912. BELOW: The first motorised mail van arrives, 3 July 1912. (EL) INSET: The former Post Office of 1911, replacing in Rolle Street that of 1878 on the Parade. (LHNB)

ABOVE: Mr Clode's pastry cooks pose in Chapel Street. (LHNB)
BELOW: Mr Ellett, insurance agent, ship broker, coal and firewood
merchant — a man for all seasons. (LHNB)

Ports of call for Edwardian housewives: ABOVE LEFT: Acland's Supply
Stores, Rolle Street, 1902; (EL) RIGHT: Allen's, butchers, High Street,
1906; (LHNB) BELOW LEFT: Clapp's bakery and cafe, Rolle Street,
damaged in the bread riots of 1867; (EL) RIGHT: Colwill's millinery and
drapery, Station Parade, c1905. (EL)

ABOVE: Open for business — Rolle Street, *c*1910. (LHNB) BELOW: A touch of class: the Imperial Hotel two years after its opening in 1869. (EL)

In Time of War

Exmouth's position, commanding the entrance to the estuary, gave it a strategic importance which its size alone would never have warranted. The earliest fort mentioned in contemporary records was one constructed in 1545 to prevent foreign vessel penetrating the Bar. Beacons on the Beacon Hill and at West Down to the east were probably part of the network planned before the Armada, but there is no specific record of their use.

In the early 17th century Exmothians were in the forefront of naval activity. In the years 1626-7 three Exmouth vessels were granted letters of marque as privateers, and three Dutch ships were taken as prizes by Captain Crosse of Exmouth in 1626. In the same year, John Drake sold the *Good Jesus*, captured by Crosse's *Willing Mind*, and in 1627 two further prizes were brought into the estuary by boats from the town.

The outbreak of Civil War in 1642 resulted in twin forts being raised by the Royalists at the river's mouth to protect the approach to Exeter. In 1643 four Parliamentary ships were trapped within the bar by contrary winds, having captured two Royalist vessels, and had 'much opposition from small guns planted at Exmouth side upon the bank or Red Cliff to the east of the church [Holy Trinity] and two planted at Star Cross, and played very hot'. Reference was also made to a small fort at 'Passage Point' on the west side of the river, garrisoned only by musketeers. In 1645 General Sir Thomas Fairfax viewed the fort at Exmouth 'which stands upon the sands and commands the passage at the mouth of the river'. In 1646 the fort was blockaded by Colonel Shapcote and surrendered after a six-week siege with 13 guns, 72 muskets and 12 barrels of powder. Captain John Gorges was appointed to command the fort in 1647, and after the Civil War was over, 'the fort in the Island of Exmouth' was repaired and garrisoned to prevent foreign landings. In 1658 Major Thomas Saunders was still trying to recover money docked from his wages when he commanded the fort at Exmouth for 16 months. It seems clear that a battery was sited at what was later known as Gun Cliff, in front of the present Louisa and Trefusis terraces, but that the principal fort controlling the river mouth stood at the northern tip of Dawlish Warren. A small sandbank called the Fort appears there on 18th century maps.

Among those who suffered for supporting Charles I during the Civil War were John Raymond of Marpool, who was fined £7 10s for being found in the besieged Exeter when it surrendered to Parliament. Another, Arthur Trevelyan of Liverton, a Roman Catholic who took up arms for the king, had his lands seized and only recovered them after ten years of litigation. Some Royalist activity was less honourable: Michael Keede of Withycombe, who rode under Sir Richard Cholmondeley, raised men and arms for the king but agreed to release some of his recruits for 5s each.

When William of Orange landed at Brixham in 1688, some of his transports are stated to have discharged their cargoes at Exmouth, and throughout the 18th century the small port witnessed a succession of naval engagements. Particularly violent conflicts followed the outbreak of war with France and Spain in 1776 and with Holland in 1780. A French privateer boarded a Scarborough collier just off the Bar in 1781, shot the mate and attempted to kill the captain, 'cutting and wounding him very much'. Although a ransom was agreed, the collier was ransacked by the French before gaining the safety of the estuary. The brig *Defiance* was stationed at Exmouth from 1782 and regularly sailed with convoys of merchant ships until succeeded by the *Helena*. In the year the *Defiance* arrived, she captured the Dutch ship *Zeuse* after a fierce battle beyond the Bar, killing some 40 of her crew, who were buried on the Warren. In May 1782 a Swedish vessel had already taken on the Exmouth pilot when she was attacked by a French cutter and three months later another Swedish ship was only spared because her French assailant had already taken two other prizes. The news of peace in 1783 was greeted in the town with 'general illumination' and other demonstrations of joy.

A battery was constructed in 1794 'on the gun point, where the old battery formerly was', after a personal visit from the Duke of Richmond — it was washed away in 1796. A signal station on West Down Beacon, similarly built in 1794, was still in use in 1816. The Napoleonic Wars were also marked by the formation of Exmouth volunteer companies, which enlivened the life of the town with their frequent balls, drills and manoeuvres on Woodbury Common. An artillery company was set up in the town in 1860 under Captain Edward Divett, MP, of Bystock, and the first guns were installed on the old site near the present lifeboat museum in that year. A battery was constructed there in 1862, although the regular firing drills with the 32- and later 36-pounders must have shattered the tranquillity of seaside life. The battery was demolished in about 1908, survived by a smaller battery sited on the Maer by 1864.

When war came again to the sea front in 1939, the beach forgot the sunny days when bathers sported in the shallows, and sprouted barbed wire, steel and concrete obstacles, with pill-boxes along the esplanade and gun emplacements at Foxholes. The precautions taken inland, graphically recorded by Eric Delderfield, included 22 air-raid shelters, the conversion of the present library into an ARP centre, and a look-out tower above Orcombe Point. Bombs were dropped on the town intermittently between 1940 and 1943, killing 56 people. The most horrific raid came on 26 February 1943, when 25 died. In 1944 the town's home guard of 800 men, which had manned the coast and cliffs waiting for the invasion that thankfully never came, was finally disbanded and the beaches cleared. The War Memorial, a reminder of those from the town who lost their lives in two World Wars, dominates the Strand Gardens.

Several Royal Navy warships which have borne the town's name also commemorate Sir Edward Pellew, the celebrated naval commander of the Napoleonic wars, who took the title Baron Exmouth in 1814 and was advanced to a Viscountcy in 1816. The first *HMS Exmouth*, a 90-gun ship, was built at Plymouth in 1841 and launched as a steam vessel in 1854. She assisted in the blockade of Russia and in bombardments during the Crimean War in 1855. Demoted to a training ship in 1875, she was sold in 1905. The battleship *Exmouth* was launched in 1901 and served as flagship to successive vice-admirals, later becoming a gunnery training ship and passing out of service in 1919. The name was next bestowed on a short-lived destroyer in 1934, a ship which was mined or torpedoed (no-one knows which) in the North Sea on 21 January 1940, with the loss of 168 lives. The present *HMS Exmouth*, a frigate, was launched in 1955, became the first Royal Naval vessel to be converted wholly to gas-turbine propulsion and was placed on the reserve list in 1976.

ABOVE: The Battery c1845, showing the coastguard station behind and Trefusis Terrace above. (EL) BELOW: Close range view of the Battery c1870. (EL) RIGHT: The proxy lord — the first Viscount Exmouth, died 1833. (MC)

91

ABOVE: Exmothians vie with each other to receive the Royal Devon Yeomanry, 1886. (LHNB) BELOW: 'Lieutenant Carter (of the Volunteers) is not aware that he is heading a procession', c1900. (WG) INSET: The end of the Great War. (EL)

92

ABOVE: Two times twelve helmets on a ground voluntary, with stirrup
pumps couchant against a trio of buckets — a splendid pattern of service
by the Exmouth Fire Guard, Albion Street area, 1939-45. (EL) BELOW:
The grim aftermath of one of the many air raids that Exmouth suffered in
the Second World War: Chapel Street area, 1941. (EL)

Littleham Church in its rural setting, by John Wallace Tucker, 1867.
Today only the church survives. (EL)

Priest and Parish

The division of the original site of Exmouth between the parishes of Littleham and Withycombe in itself betrays the town's more recent foundation. Before the Reformation — indeed, before the Norman Conquest — much of the area of these two parishes was held by religious houses, and these monasteries would have regarded the spiritual welfare of their tenants as a moral duty.

A church in Littleham village, dedicated to St Andrew, almost certainly existed in Saxon times; both Horton and (from 1139) Sherborne Abbey probably served the parish with monks from their own cloisters. The traffic was a two-way one, for Roger de Littleham was a Sherborne monk in 1242. During a vacancy in the Sherborne abbacy in 1213, King John gave Littleham church to Nicholas de Adham, a clerk, for life, and it was probably as a result of this grant that the bishop of Exeter laid hands on it. In 1234 the bishop, with or without Sherborne's consent, gave the church to the dean and chapter of Exeter Cathedral. Ever since, the chapter has appointed the vicars of Littleham, who sought the salvation of their flock for a stipend of £5 a year in the 13th century.

Although Withycombe was both a civil and ecclesiastical parish, its church, mentioned in 1289, was by 1291 a chapelry dependent on East Budleigh church. Dedicated to St John the Baptist by 1414, it has more recently been known as St John's in the Wilderness, allegedly because of its isolated position. The dependence on Budleigh meant that services in Withycombe were the responsibility of East Budleigh's vicar, or of curates appointed and paid by him, in return for which he received the small tithes. The great tithes, including those on grain, formed the rectory estate of Withycombe, which was held with East Budleigh and Bystock property by Polsloe Priory under a grant from Prince (later King) John. After the Dissolution, they were purchased in turn by the Drake and Duke families.

When Exmouth developed around the ferry station in the 12th and 13th centuries, the journey from Pratteshide to St John's or Littleham was hazardous, and in 1329 the lord of Hille was allowed a chapel at Pratteshide — probably, but not certainly, on the site of St Margaret's Chapel at the junction of Chapel and Margaret streets. This chapel is known to have been built by 1375, when a cottage on the site of the Volunteer Inn was described as being opposite St Margaret's, and in 1381 the chapel was re-licensed by the bishop. The building was converted to a house in 1724 and occupied by a tailor in 1744. The piscina for holy water was fixed in the west wall and in 1760 was most inappropriately used as a punch bowl to drink the new king's health. When the building was demolished in 1961, fragments of 14th century window tracery and worked stone were found, although little of the original structure survived. It may have been the demise of St Margaret's which led to its dedication being added to that of St Andrew at Littleham.

As the mediaeval village expanded further into Littleham parish, around the Strand and up the northern and western slopes of Chapel Hill, a chapel was needed on the other side of the boundary. In 1348 Walter Cok endowed the newly-erected chapel of St Saviour at Chickstone with a house and one virgate of land, probably to accommodate the chaplain who served there. Its exact site is unknown, but it had been demolished by the Reformation; it was evidently superseded in 1412 by a second chapel on Chapel Hill, dedicated to the Holy Trinity. This was the only such building in the Exmouth area to have a tower, and as well as housing three bells, it served as a seamark and look-out point.

By 1414 St Margaret's was evidently too small for the inhabitants on the older side of the town; possibly they were jealous of the new and larger Holy Trinity Chapel. In a petition to the Pope, they complained that people in the western part of Exmouth, probably those living immediately south of the present Parade, were cut off by the sea from St John's. They added that in winter the floods were so great and the road so muddy and rocky that the dead could not be carried thither for burial, children were denied christening and women were not churched. Even when they could make the journey, they were afraid lest pirates should take the town and burn it. They asked to build a chapel dedicated to St Anne and permission was granted for a chapel with font, bell-tower and cemetery. There is no evidence that it was ever built. The last mediaeval chapel erected was St Michael's, in the village of Bradham by 1435, more recently known as Withycombe village.

Thus the growing settlement at the river's mouth had no resident vicar. Although its chapels catered to certain needs of the community, come Sunday or Holy Day, Exmothians were expected to undertake the long trek into the hinterland to make their devotions. The situation was even worse at Bystock, a detached part of Colaton Raleigh parish, where in 1819 the owner, Edward Divett, complained that 'my parish church is absolutely inaccessible to my family, five miles on Devonshire's roads being little better than a pilgrimage'. If that could be said of Bystock in the 19th century, how much worse must Exmouth's position have been in the Middle Ages.

The result of such clerical isolation was that Exmouth was poorly served by underpaid curates or sometimes not served at all. The vicar of Littleham sat in his vicarage at Littleham opposite the east end of the church, and his relationship with his parishioners in the neighbouring town inevitably suffered. Even at Littleham the vicar was not invariably respected. In 1613 Simon Peake was accused of allowing the vicarage to fall into disrepair, of not preaching regularly on Sundays, and 'for that he doth hunt and use alehouses disorderly'. A bequest by Robert Drake for an Exmouth lecturer in 1628 was intended to improve the situation, but the money had found its way into the vicar's pocket by 1656. In that year, Trinity Chapel was described as 'nowe in very great ruine and decay, the lead which covered the same being cutt off, the timber work destroyed'.

In 1664 the then vicar, Daniel Moore, was transferred elsewhere by Bishop Ward, who believed that he would 'doe but little good by his ministry' because of 'differences and animosities' with his parishioners. In 1779 Vicar John Fortescue did not even live at Littleham but at Topsham, which he also held, totally blind and unable to celebrate divine service.

Withycombe continued to be served from East Budleigh vicarage until the two were finally separated as late as 1850. Curates did duty in north Exmouth only as long as Budleigh vicars were prepared to pay their salaries, and no house was provided for them. Vicar Benjamin Jouxson was suspended in 1724 when he tried to dispossess his Withycombe curate, William Gillett, and Matthew Mundy, vicar from 1741, did without a curate altogether. He was notorious for breaking off in the middle of his Withycombe sermons to ride post-haste to preach at Budleigh. It was also he who demolished the south aisle and chancel of St John's in 1788, sold the bells and allegedly pocketed the proceeds. It was not until 1926 that work to repair his ravages started, and the completed church was reconsecrated in 1937.

When improvements came, they were engineered by the laity. In 1722 Sir John Colleton paid for the rebuilding of St Michael's Chapel; Holy Trinity, being 'too small to contain the inhabitants', was rebuilt in 1779 on Chapel Hill, and extended in 1798 by the addition of a semi-circular south aisle. Holy Trinity, the only place of worship in the expanding urban area, rapidly became the centre of religious life. In the first 40 years of the 19th century, Exmouth's population almost doubled, and many a victory procession, masonic gathering and school crocodile wound its way thither. By 1818 Trinity had overflowed again and in 1824 a new stately church rose upon the Beacon Fields, thanks wholly to Lord Rolle's generosity. Even with Rolle's help, money was in short supply and the old barrel organ served for two years until a new instrument was ceremonially 'played in' by Mr Salter from Exeter Cathedral. The church authorities finally came to terms with the town's expansion and, when the old Trinity Chapel was demolished in 1827, a new vicarage rose phoenix-like upon the hill — and the vicar came in from Littleham at last.

At this time the vicar was John Rymer, instituted in 1803. In 1806 he was involved in an unseemly argument at Littleham with his parish clerk, over fees for a wedding he was celebrating. These had been paid to the clerk and not the vicar. Rymer threw off his surplice and refused to perform the ceremony, which duly landed him in the bishop's Consistory Court. While preaching in Holy Trinity's pulpit in 1808, he rebuked a trio of young ladies who were misbehaving themselves and found himself up in front of the bishop again, an ordeal from which death released him in less than a year. His two successors were non-resident, but T. J. Rocke, vicar 1843-77, came here at a time when the Anglican Church was searching for its identity. In 1851 Rocke suffered a meeting in Littleham vestry to protest against his alleged Tractarian practices, and although he promptly ejected his opponents, it proved less easy to silence the wagging of their powerful tongues. One wit commented in 1861 that the town had built its houses upon the sand but founded its church upon a Rocke.

Holy Trinity gained a chancel in 1855, provided by Lady Rolle, but the Beer stone of the fabric rotted and in the years 1905-7 it assumed its present form, with the addition of a transept and Lady Chapel.

In Withycombe parish, a gallery was added to St Michael's in 1814 and the nearby church of St John the Evangelist was consecrated in 1864. A small former Wesleyan chapel at the end of Hall's Place was taken over by the Anglicans in 1888 and dedicated to St Margaret. Enlarged, it was used until the opening of All Saints' Church on Exeter Road in 1898. St Margaret's subsequently became the present Royal Cinema. In Littleham, St Saviour's Mission Chapel was established in 1881, St Andrew's Church succeeded a similar mission chapel in 1896 and St Mary's in Hamilton Lane opened about 1932. Since 1972 the two parishes of Littleham and Withycombe have worked closely together under team ministries handled by their respective rectors, although there is still no parish of Exmouth as such.

Such neglect by the Anglican Church would have led, in most other south-western towns, to the development by the mid-17th century of a powerful dissenting faction, probably with left-wing politics. This did not happen here, possibly because Exmouth was still only a village, with a shifting male population, many of whom would have been at sea at any one time. The nearest dissenting chapel was set up at Gulliford in Lympstone after the Toleration Act of 1689; its registers survive only from 1773, but it seems to have been little used by Exmouth people. Its burial ground survives, but the only influential Exmothians who travelled thither to worship were the Giffords of Cliff End House (now the Park Hotel).

Taking Withycombe parish as an example, the vicar of Budleigh reported in 1744 that there were only five Presbyterian families out of a total of 80, and by 1764 even this number had declined to one or two. The result of neglect was not a radical population but, among the working classes, an irreligious one. An Exeter gentleman considered the town of 1776 to be 'so wicked a place' that even nonconformity was unlikely to gain a toe-hold. But time was to prove that it was an evangelical message which would appeal to the labourers, sailors and tradesmen of the town. In 1776 Wilhelmina, Vicountess Glenorchy, brought her chaplain to preach at Exmouth and, although ejected from the Long Room at the Globe by Samuel Eyre, a local Justice, within a year they had established an Independent (later Congregational) Chapel behind Mona Island in Exeter Road. The first two pastors together served the chapel for 85 years: Robert Winton from 1776 to 1818 and Richard Clapson from 1820 to'63. The chapel had a burial ground by 1784 and a Sunday School from 1817, and was rebuilt in 1866, although the Ilfracombe builder went bankrupt during the course of the contract.

In 1806, after a dispute with Robert Winton, a splinter group led by Richard Staple broke away to worship in Bicton Place, building a brick meeting-house in 1810. It was known as the Ebenezer Chapel but colloquially rechristened 'the Little Revenge'. Enlarged in 1828, it briefly closed in 1855, because the congregation disapproved of its minister wearing a white hat 'as it did not look clerical'. The Beacon Congregational Church, as it was later known, was rebuilt in 1893, but in more recent times was closed to become an overalls factory, and replaced in 1955 by a United Reformed Church at Littleham on the Salterton Road. The 150-year-old rift was mended by naming the new building 'Glenorchy'.

The Wesleyan Methodists arrived rather late in the town, in 1808. Meeting first near Glenorchy Chapel, they transferred to Fore Street and in 1843-4 built a chapel on the Parade. In 1858 a division of opinion, to which the 19th century Free Churches were unduly susceptible, led to the Primitive Methodists retaining the Parade chapel, rebuilt in 1890. After occupying a succession of homes, the Wesleyans built a new chapel in Brunswick (now Windsor) Square in 1872, and in 1895 moved to their present church in Tower Street. The Windsor Square chapel, renamed Christ Church, was taken over by the Reformed Episcopal Church, a local breakaway group from the Anglicans, later known as the Free Church of England. A Wesleyan chapel, established in Withycombe village in 1884, was rebuilt in 1907, and the Littlemead Methodist Church was opened at Roundhouse Lane in 1968.

The Plymouth Brethren met in the town from 1843, causing a public sensation in 1860, when they tried to baptise eleven converts in the sea on an ebb tide. Their Zion Chapel in Margaret Street was succeeded in 1872 by the present Gospel Hall in Exeter Road. The Baptists came to the town in 1891, building their church in Victoria Road in 1900, and setting up the Brixington Free Church in Churchill Road in 1972. The Exmouth Independent Evangelical Church in Scott Drive was founded in 1967. Other sects, such as the Society of Friends, Salvation Army, Sanctuary of the Spirit, Jehovah's Witnesses and Christian Scientists, have also established themselves in Exmouth.

The Roman Catholics celebrated mass from 1887 at the present Park Hotel in Exeter Road, then a private house called the Lawn. A temporary church was built in the garden of a house in Windsor Square in 1891, replaced in 1914 by the Church of the Holy Ghost in Raddenstile Lane. The new Church of St Anne on the Brixington estate has provided a home for the piscina from the mediaeval St Margaret's Chapel.

The slim survivor of what was once a much larger St John's, 1902.
(LHNB)

ABOVE: 19th c. interior of Littleham Church before restoration in 1883-4.
(EL) BELOW: St John's in 1910. (LHNB)

100

ABOVE: An early watercolour of St John's in the Wilderness, (EL) and
BELOW: the second Holy Trinity on Chapel Hill, 1805, with the Manor
House on the left. (EL)

101

ABOVE: A last look at Trinity Chapel after closure and before
demolition in 1827. The foreground is dominated by the lodge to the
main Temple in the later Imperial grounds. The lodge was modelled on
the Temple of the Winds at Athens. (EL) BELOW: John Pitch's design
for Holy Trinity, 1823. (EL)

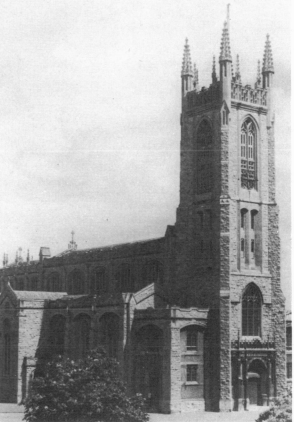

ABOVE: The finished article: Holy Trinity 1824. (EL)   LEFT: The
interior, with three-decker pulpit and galleries, since removed, c1855.
(EL) RIGHT: Trinity today. (EL)

103

ABOVE LEFT: St Michael's Chapel, With
the tomb of Sir John Colleton. (EL) CEN
foundation stone of the Church of St John
RIGHT: Robert Winton, private schoolm
1801. (EL) BELOW, FAR LEFT: the fade
replacement, 1866. (EL) LEFT: Christ Ch
Zion Chapel, Margaret Street, demolishe
Exeter Road c1890, (LHNB) and FAR RIG
Lane, 1960. (EL)   BELOW: The firs
                    Baker, died 26 Nove

104

...lt 1720, in 1836; in the foreground, ... of stovepipes: Lady Rolle lays the ...elist at Withycombe, 21 July 1864. ...st minister of Glenorchy, taken in ...Glenorchy Chapel, on the point of ...ndsor Square. (LHNB) CENTRE: ...NB) RIGHT: the Gospel Hall in ...rch of the Holy Ghost, Raddenstile ...the Ebenezer Chapel, John Peck ...aged 66. (EL)

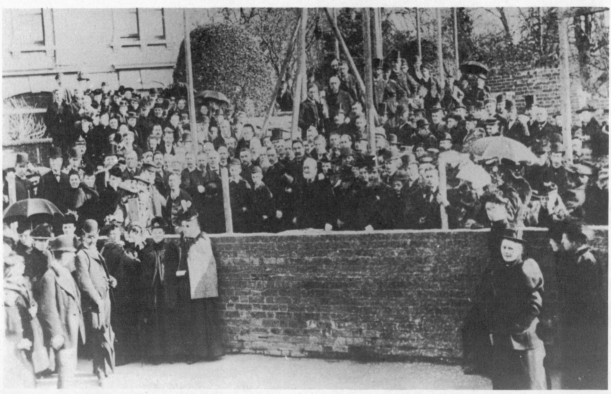

ABOVE: Wesleyan meeting house at the bottom of Tower Street, before the Methodist Chapel was built there in 1895. (EL) BELOW: A Christian society builds for the future; the Exmouth Freemasons lay the foundation stone of their hall in St Andrew's Road, 1894. (EL)

Just Deserts

The men and women of Exmouth were probably no more and no less law-abiding than other Devonians, but few other areas could boast of having attracted a 13th century private detective. Thus it was in 1263 when Henry de Bratton came to Littleham to investigate the theft of the abbot of Sherborne's goods there. We are not told if the culprits were brought to book, but John Tubbe was certainly fortunate in 1296 when, after he killed Mariota Uppehille with a stick at Merpole (Marpool), the verdict was accidental death.

Areas along the coast were in constant danger from pirates and in 1329 two ships, the *Cogg Nostre Dame* and the *Rode Cogg*, both of Exmouth, were 'taken by certain evildoers of the power of the king of France'. Such piracy continued into the 18th century, boats from North Africa seizing many a defenceless vessel. In 1400 Walter Levenant, a clergyman, complained that a gang, including no less than three parsons, had burgled his house and broken into his fields at Littleham, lain in ambush to kill him and assaulted and threatened his servants so that they were afraid to till his crops. It was probably a member of the same family, Robert Levenant, lessee of Littleham rectory lands and half Littleham manor, who fled and was outlawed in 1409.

Piracy could work two ways, and an Exmouth mariner, William Keede, was accused in 1430 of seizing near Guernsey a ship loaded at Brittany, in 1431 with other Exmothians of taking ships of Rouen and Brittany, and in 1436 of participating in an expedition with eight barges against a Breton port. On this last occasion they had carried off to Plymouth a ship laden with Rochelle wine, 24 flitches of bacon and 7 fur mantles. The tables were turned in 1452 when Keede's Exmouth house was burgled and 800 lb of iron stolen.

Assault was all too common in the 15th century, and the hundred court in particular dealt with a surprising number of cases. In 1455 John Riggeway was prosecuted for attacking the tithingman with a dagger and taking a horse from him, although the unfortunate officer was fined for not producing the dagger in evidence. The women of Exmouth were also endowed with hot tempers: Alice Baker insulted Robert Mixbur in 1461 and went for him with a cornpike. The weapons used in such assaults at this time included stones, swords, pitchforks, axes and even, in 1453, a cockle rake. Other crimes were lesser; John Glasier allowing his pigs to stray in the streets unringed in 1452, Robert Crofteman swearing at the tithingman in 1454 while his wife gave the king's bailiff similar treatment, John Mychell taking Thomas Snellyng's chickens at Withycombe in 1566, Alexander Kymer in the following year accusing Gilbert Drake, gentleman, of altering the Littleham church books when the fancy took him, and Richard Whitbourne, the famous navigator, prosecuting Robert Newcombe for trespassing on his lands in 1594.

Exmothians could also find themselves hauled up before one of the six manor courts. In 1629 Littleham court fined William Hooper for harbouring Charles, a Frenchman, and the same court prosecuted his children as common hedge breakers. The manor courts were obliged to maintain a cucking stool, for ducking shrewish women, and stocks, both of which the reeve of Littleham had to supply in 1637, using timber provided by the lord of the manor. Indeed, the threat of confinement in the stocks was heard in an Exmouth Petty Sessions court as late as 1860. George Symons of Withycombe was set in the stocks for three hours in 1626 for abusing the constable, although in 1641 Gabriel and Margaret Short were let off with a fine of 13s 4d as long as they confessed their faults at Littleham church's lych gate. The puritanical regime which followed the Civil War had its own consequences, as when George Heyman, a Littleham farmer, was prosecuted at Quarter Sessions for setting up a maypole and insulting the constables who told him to remove it.

The parish registers of Littleham record the sad end of some Exmothians: William Nicholls, hanged in 1631, Thomas Lee, found shot beneath the cliff in 1657, Mary wife of William Hooper, who killed herself in 1670 by 'ripping open her belley and tareing her gutts in peeces', and Sarah Lloyd, shot by her sweetheart in 1781. Life was harsh and punishments cruel. In 1770 John Andrews was transported to the colonies for stealing £12 from Mary Richards' house at Exmouth. An apprentice who ran away from his master before his time was up could be forcibly returned and any person who took him in prosecuted. In 1770 Thomas Bellamy fled from his master, who advertised in the Exeter newspaper for his return, describing him as 19 years old, 5 ft tall, wearing a blue jacket, red waistcoat and white trousers, and having an impediment in his speech.

Hardship led men to desperate acts. One of the saddest stories is that of William Pomeroy. Starting out in life as butler to the Ducarel family at the Manor House on Chapel Hill, he had become inn-keeper at the Golden Lion by 1779 and moved to the Globe in 1783. The lavish balls that he mounted for the gentry failed to bring him the profits he sought and in 1798 he went bankrupt. The lease of the Globe, four post chaises, a hearse and all his 'elegant household goods' right down to the fire irons and fenders came under the hammer. Finally, on the evening of 7 March 1800, he attempted to hold up a chaise driven by his son and carrying his former master, Philip Ducarel, to steal the payroll of the Lympstone Volunteers. After a scuffle, during which his pistol misfired several times, he was recognised and escaped into the night, never to be heard of again.

War with France meant French prisoners of war, and Exmouth provided the perfect escape route for them. Three prisoners who absconded from Ashburton in 1778 were discovered on board two Dutch vessels in the estuary. In 1800 another band of escapees stole a yacht but ran aground on the Bar, using the ship's boat to get as far as Dartmouth, where they were recaptured. Only two weeks later, others stole John Ball's fishing boat, 'the poor man's all', and got clean away. Several French officers, armed with cutlasses, broke their parole at Crediton in 1807 and, prevented by one valiant mariner from taking his boat on the beach, coolly took another. One Frenchman, François Farre, ended up at the Assizes in 1812 for audaciously trying to steal the Exmouth pilot boat.

Nineteenth century Exmouth was a relatively law-abiding place. In the hundred years between 1760 and 1860 only three murders were recorded and one of these, that of an Exmouth member of a naval press gang in 1803, took place on Dawlish Warren. Another, of the steward of a revenue cutter who was thought to have drowned, only came to light 20 years after the event in 1855, when a London woman confessed to the guilty secret on her death bed. The third was that of William Goat, found dead near the customs house on the Point in 1838. In no case is the culprit known to have been brought to book. Most crimes were of a more minor variety, as when Sir Walter Roberts' postillion at Courtlands put a noxious substance, cantharides, in the tea before absconding in 1822, or in the case of John

Long, who attempted to steal lead from the roof of one of Lord Rolle's Exmouth houses in 1826.

Some cases were totally ludicrous: in 1842 an Exmouth gentleman, John Wise of Highfield House, was invited to dinner with an absent-minded Sidmouth doctor, and finding his host out, gave vent to his frustration by throwing stones through the windows. Similarly, in 1849, a labourer, Francis England, when ordered to dispose of his pig which was causing a nuisance at Withycombe, asked for a stay of execution so that he might fatten it up before selling it. When the renewal of the Pilot Inn's licence was contested in 1850, Isaac Rake, the local constable, testified that it was the landlord's misfortune 'to have a drunken wife who made more noise than all the frequenters of the house'. Most of the perennial court appearances concerned drinking, but the charge of harbouring a police officer while on duty was a rare one; Thomas Shapter, landlord of the Anchor, was fined 15s for allowing PC Brook to play bagatelle with a railway porter. Sometimes disagreements arose between innkeepers, as when the landlord of the York Hotel was fined 5s for the delight of throwing a bucket of water over the landlord's daughter from the South-Western Hotel in 1863. Two years later, the new-fangled telegraph was used to arrest a sailor at Salisbury who had stolen the 'fancy dog' kept by that same landlord of the York.

The Petty Sessions for Woodbury division were held, like so many official functions, at the Globe Hotel; after its demolition in 1866, they took place behind Balcony House near Manchester Quay, and later at the Public Hall (now the Savoy Cinema) in Rolle Street. The police, who succeeded the old parish constables, were accommodated in South Street until a new police station was built in 1914 in Victoria Road, in 1969 replaced by its successor in Windsor Square.

Misdeeds were in most cases prompted less by inherent wickedness than by deprivation, for behind the gloss and glitter of a fashionable resort, as in any other English town, the less fortunate lived a life of uncertainty and often cruel hardship. A prolonged period of bad weather, which prevented the fishing fleet from putting to sea, an outbreak of war, which closed export markets and made dangerous seas even more hazardous, a severe winter, or a failed harvest — all these could bring hunger and ruin in their wake.

The two parishes and their officers at first carried the burden of caring for the poor, but when disasters like the plague struck, a wider region was called upon for aid. Thus in 1628 additional rates were collected from the five neighbouring hundreds for the relief of Exmouth, and by April there were 300 sick here with the dreaded disease. Littleham's register records the progress of the plague, often showing that the dead could not be carried to the parish church for burial, but were interred on Chapel Hill or even at the roadside. Not until July 1629 was the town free of the pestilence.

It was probably the same visitation which in September 1628 carried off Robert Drake of Dalditch, who left, among many charitable bequests, 40s a year each for the poor of Littleham, Withycombe and East Budleigh to be distributed three times a year, and 20s to wine and dine those who turned up for the annual audit. He also left £5 a year to bind out poor apprentices of the two Exmouth parishes, relieve poor tradesmen and employ those out of work. There was £20 to build an almshouse at Withycombe, which survived near St Michael's until 1909, and probably succeeded an earlier almshouse in Bradham, held in 1567 by Barnard Drake. A further £7 a year went towards a dinner on the Sunday after Lady Day for twelve of the founder's relations, later known as the Mess of the Kinsfolk and celebrated until the late 18th century. Over the years these funds have supplemented those doled out by the overseers of the poor and churchwardens.

In Littleham in 1630 the churchwardens paid small sums to several travellers, including a gentlewoman of Ireland, seven poor sailors and a poor man and his wife, and in 1638 five Frenchmen managed to milk the parish to the tune of 1s 6d. Again in 1638 they paid for stripping the corpse and supplying a shroud for a drowned man and, because life must go on, provided beer for those who did the job. There were three poor sailors who had lost their ship, a Plymouth boy coming from Dunkirk, and three soldiers from Flanders, all in 1641. The wardens were not going to risk a bastard child from Topsham settling in their midst and paid as much as 9s 11d in 1658 to send the infant back again, while eight poor castaway seamen only merited 8s nine years later. A correspondent writing in 1666 referred to 'the great necessities of this poore towne', stating that 'the poore there are very clamerous'.

The scale of the problem is indicated by the Withycombe overseers' accounts. In 1713 they spent over £40 on the poor, relieving 13 regular paupers and buying sheets, shirts and shifts for those who could not afford them, including a coat and breeches for John Stoning and an apron for Bridget Bence. The following year four paupers fell sick, and Dr Symonds earned himself £4 5s for medicines. The learned doctor was a regular recipient, getting £1 for Stephen Hopping's leg and 14s for Walter Taylor's 'disorder', although it was a Dr Bennett who secured two guineas for curing Baggs' leg.

Public subscriptions became popular for dealing with extraordinary problems, like the high price of food during the Napoleonic Wars. In 1801 such a subscription was started to buy wheat, barley and potatoes for resale to the poor at lower prices. In the same year, the ending of the war by the French surrender in Egypt was celebrated by providing the poor with an ox, bread, two hogsheads of cider and two of beer; George III's Jubilee in 1809 resulted in a dance, sports and a feast for the poor on the lawns at Marpool, and after heavy snow in 1814, the gentry distributed money and coal. The less fortunate must often have prayed for victories, not out of patriotism but because it might result in full bellies. In one week during the violent cholera outbreak of 1832, 922 quarts of strong soup and 92½ lbs of meat, as well as brandy, wine and arrowroot, were doled out. Lord Rolle was not to be outdone by his contemporaries and at Christmas that year he handed over two fat bullocks and supplied 200 poor families with blankets, flannels and stockings. The Coronation of 1838 brought a further subscription meal for 1,500 people. The high cost of bread in 1847 led to a riot by 500 people, who broke into bakers' shops and elicited yet another subscription to quieten them. This was a time of popular revolutions in Europe and the English gentry were concerned that the poor should be kept relatively contented. Such measures, however, failed to prevent a similar attack on bakers' and butchers' shops in 1867.

Parochial responsibility for the poor ended in 1836 when Littleham and Withycombe became part of the St Thomas Poor Law Union. Thereafter, and well into the present century, paupers were sent to the Union workhouse near Exeter and thus divorced from their homes, family and friends. For some it must have been the longest journey they ever made; for many it was their last.

Concern over the health and sanitation of the town, following the Public Health Act of 1848, led to a public enquiry a year later. It was principally concerned with the drainage of some 170 houses into the area within Hull's embankment to the west of Exeter Road, an area now known as the Colony, then as the Marsh or, more evocatively, the Green Slime. This region dried out in summer, when 'the odour was horrible' in the fashionable houses built along the Parade — and even further away when a breeze blew in from the river.

Thomas Eustace, a surgeon, described the town as 'the worst, dirtiest town in the county'. Elizabeth Dyer, living on Manchester Quay, spoke of a drain running underneath her house covered only with large stones, of the smell which penetrated her floorboards, and how she had to unblock the choked channel herself. The nearby pump was polluted by the sea and water for tea had to be fetched from a considerable distance.

John Land, another surgeon, described South Street as the poorest area, where the filth of 40 to 50 houses was dumped in back yards or in the street and the nearest pump was in Fore Street. The poor even stored their ordure so that they could sell it as manure at up to 4s a load. Mortality that year was nearly twice the average and there had been twelve deaths from scarlet fever in three months. The inspector, summing up, reported that he had 'never yet seen human habitations more devoid of the precautions necessary for the preservation of health and cleanliness — more crowded, dark, close, filthy, and loathsome' than those in South Town and the adjoining streets.

The net result came in 1850 with the formation of the Local Board of Health, which duly appointed an inspector of nuisances and a scavenger or refuse collector. Drains were improved, the Brixham Brook was to be diverted to flush out the Marsh, and a hundred and one orders went out to reconstruct privies, expel pigs, repair roads and clear drains. Little improvement in general health could be expected until fresh water was brought into the town. A water company had been formed as early as 1842 and a reservoir was built in 1849 in Brunswick Square, on the site of the present police station. Unfortunately the scheme was not popular; there was insufficient pressure to force the water beyond the ground floor of houses, and few took advantage of it. A new Act to bring water from Squabmoor on Woodbury Common was passed in 1864, but the work took three years to complete, partly because the contractor refused to carry out the engineer's plans. The company was finally taken over by the Urban District Council in 1902, and a new borehole at Dotton was opened by Lady Clinton in 1911 — after some five years of violent disagreement. A further borehole and reservoir at Dotton were completed in 1952.

A public dispensary was established at Manchester House in 1868 and later moved to Church Street, but most patients had to travel to Exeter for treatment until the Maud Hospital was founded in Clarence Road by Mrs Hume Long in 1884. Moved to the top of Bicton Street in 1886, it was taken over by the town in 1900. The building proved inadequate and the present Hospital in Claremont Grove was completed in 1903, extended and remodelled in 1928. A health centre has recently been added.

Gas lighting had come to the town in 1842 to shed embarrassing light on its cobbled streets, and on a modern note, consumers held a meeting at the London Inn as early as 1851 to protest at its high price. A supply of electricity was proposed in 1899, but works at Marpool were not completed until 1913. The telephone came privately at first, as an exchange of 24 lines established by a local doctor in Rolle Road; a few years later, in 1894, the town was linked to the South Devon and Exeter line of the National Telephone Company. Another means of communication, the newspaper, came in 1853 when the *Exmouth Mercury* was founded. It was joined by the *Exmouth Journal*, founded by Thomas Freeman in 1858 — both were Conservative papers. The *Exmouth Chronicle* was instituted by a Liberal, George Setten, in 1882. The *Journal*, still issued from its original offices on Chapel Hill, has successively and successfully absorbed both its rivals.

The Board of Health built new sewers in 1861 to improve the town's drainage, adding an outfall at Maer Rocks, completed in 1883. Further schemes were required in 1899, completed in 1902, and again in 1932. The work of the Board was greatly assisted by the

Rolle Estate Act of 1865. Until that date, leases had been granted for the lives of three nominated persons, and in a world where disease could easily wipe out a family, this offered little incentive for the improvement of property. Thereafter leases were granted for 99 years absolute and the trustees of the estate were also empowered to make public improvements — a clause which permitted the building of Rolle Street.

Apart from the Guardians of the Poor Law Union, the Board of Health ruled Exmouth for nearly half a century, only replaced in 1894 by the Exmouth Urban District Council. In its turn, the Council watched over the growing town for 80 years until that fateful day, 1 April 1974, when local government was 'reorganised'. Exmouth had been the largest town in the old administrative county. With the creation of the East Devon District Council, seated at Sidmouth, the town has been left without a voice of its own, a voice to declare its hopes and its fears for the future. True, an Exmouth Town Committee now meets, but it is without teeth and can only advise and recommend. Perhaps one day the town will again be able to determine its own destiny.

Exmouth's educational needs are much better safeguarded and have a most respectable pedigree. Robert Drake, founder of charities, also left £7 a year by his will of 1628 to pay a lecturer and schoolmaster in Littleham and Exmouth, adding that the first master should be the curate, George Codner. The bequest was paid irregularly, for a 17th century petition from the inhabitants declared that since the death of John Carnell no school had been kept for 18 years. William Coleman was licensed to teach grammar here in 1644, and after the Civil War, William Bence taught an English school under the Drake charity. At the same time Edmond Daye taught in Littleham, a man who had suffered during the war 'by plunder and other calamaties incident to loyalty'. In 1663 Exmothians petitioned the bishop that Daye might be licensed to teach 'writing and siphering, which is useful and requisite for the children of Exmouth'. The following year the bishop decided that £7 was too small a sum to employ both a schoolmaster and lecturer and decreed that there should be either one or the other. Thereafter a succession of licences was issued to schoolmasters, but by 1694 none could be found. The money was consequently paid to the vicar of Littleham, who was presumably expected to lecture for it, and the same arrangement was confirmed to the next two vicars in 1706 and 1723, and apparently to their successors.

With the development of the watering place a rash of private schools for young ladies and gentlemen sprang up. From 1786 Robert Winton, the Independent minister, instructed boys in English, Latin and Greek for 18 guineas a year, including board and lodging. Two years later, the Rev H. Mugg offered to teach six young hopefuls such exotic subjects as elocution, orthography, merchants' accounts and the use of globes. Ladies were catered for by Mrs Cooke (died 1818) in Fore Street from 1795, and at Mrs Langworthy's seminary in 1801, where a Parisian lady who had fled from the French Revolution was engaged to teach her native tongue. A dancing academy was opened at the London Hotel in 1808, tutored by Mr Diot from Exeter. By 1830 there were five private schools, by 1848 there were ten, and in 1857 eleven.

Attention turned to the education of the poor when Lord and Lady Rolle founded a National School in Little Bicton Place for 200 children. Annual sermons were preached for its support, in 1833 by the bishop himself, and treats arranged for the children, such as beef and plum pudding at the Globe in 1829, or even strong beer to celebrate the Coronation of 1831. The school sermon was preached in 1839 by Dr E. B. Pusey, a founder of the Oxford Movement. Similar National Schools had been established at Withycombe by 1860 and at Littleham by 1861. Plans for a new Exmouth school were launched in 1860, when the existing building was overflowing with 270 pupils. Fund-raising events included a bazaar held on the Temple lawns in 1863 with four marquees, including a museum and a post office. The new school buildings, sited nearby in Little Bicton Place, are still in use today. One fondly remembered teacher, John Bannister, who held sway between 1869 and 1906, had followed his father, who retired in 1859 because of failing sight.

A School Board, formed in 1875, erected new schools in Exeter Road and a Grammar School was established in Gypsy Lane in 1921. Senior Secondary Schools were opened at Brankscombe Park in 1936. In recent years the new Comprehensive School, based on the former Grammar and Secondary foundations, has become the largest in the kingdom, with 138 teachers and 2,500 pupils. A teachers' training college was established in 1948 and christened Rolle College. Initially for women but subsequently mixed, it has successfully survived recent cuts in higher education.

Poverty breeds crime: the Exmouth Friendly Society believed in self-help against poverty, and also enjoyed themselves — on the Parade, 1892. (EL)

ABOVE: For those who did fall on hard times, the South Street soup kitchen provided sustenance as late as the 1930s. (EL) BELOW: In 1903, the Cottage Hospital replaced the one-time private Maud Hospital. (LHNB)

ABOVE: Home of law and order — the former police station on the corner of South Street, *c*1900. (LHNB) BELOW: Its replacement on Victoria Road, built 1914, closed 1969. (EL)

EXMOUTH STAKES 1866.

No. 1.---PARSONAGE HORSE.

A rather dark steed, possessing good points, his chief weakness lies in the pertinacity with which his friends match him in races to which he is not suited; did they confine him to courses which his early training suits, he would no doubt come out a first class.

No. 2.---LITTLE CHAMPION.

A plucky colt, full of fire and mettle : there is great confidence in this colt, his friends feel certain he is just suited to the work and that he will be a winner.

No. 3.---EXMOUTH HERO.

Rather full of flesh, comes up bouncing, scarcely known so much as his good points entitle him to be.

No. 4.---OLD ENGLISH GENTLEMAN.

A very fine horse, and a good sample of breeding, has won golden opinions at times, but has one bad fault; a tendency to hold his head to high, this renders him liable to a bad fall.

No. 5.---PUFF PASTE.

A description of this horse would be useless—has no chance of winning.

No. 6.---PESTLE AND MORTAR.

A meagre looking horse, it is thought his groom Physics him to much, a very expensive horse to keep; no one thinks that he will win.

EXMOUTH LOCAL BOARD
ATHLETIC SPORTS 1871

Refreshment Bulk.
No. 1 BATTERY.

The Mayor of Exmouth, Purveyor to the King of the Cannibal Islands, begs respectfully to inform the Nobility, Ladies, and Public in general that he has received the appointment to the above Restaurant and is ready to supply Oyster Patties, Pickled mussels, Mutton pies, Potted perriwinkles & crabs, Cock soup, Hashes, made at the shortest notice.

Blacking, Hair Oil and other Vegetables, Sausage Rolls, Mulligatawny, Ladies' frizzled Rolls made to measurement, Turtle, Ox Tail, Tripe and other Soups, Hung Beef, Game in abundance, Asses' Milk for Invalids, Jelly and Cow heels, Best London Glue, Meat Pies, Magpies, &c.,--Emigrants to Portland or Dartmoor fitted out.

A Lecture on Exmouth and other parts of the county of Devon from the deluge to the present time delivered every evening.

The holder of a Grog ticket for the benefit of the Lecturer will admit the holder free.

REGISTERY OFFICE FOR FEMALES REQUIRING UNDER SITUATIONS.

Itch cured in One Hour, and Cattle Medicine.

N.B Charles Ankles Esq. has been appointed Steward.

£100 REWARD.

Missing; from his Seat on the Bench at the Exmouth Local Board of Health, GENERAL PILL-GARLIC-PESTLE-AND MORTAR; supposed to have received an appointment from the King of Ape's Island to head the mob to fight the Monkeys, or personating the Spider Ape at the Regent's Park Zoological Gardens, London.

WHOEVER will restore him to his former position, or bring him either to the **BRIBERY COLT, KING-LOBSTER TERRACE**, or to **MR. MUM**, at his Chambers, Exmouth, will receive the above Reward.

TOP and ABOVE LEFT: The going was rough if you wanted to serve the town on the local Board of Health in 1866, 1871 and on another unspecified occasion. (EL) ABOVE RIGHT: Good health extends beyond Holman and Ham's pharmacy at the foot of Chapel Hill, as the town goes on the main sewer, c1902. (EL)

117

ABOVE: Calm waters as the sewage outfall is relaid off Maer Rocks, 1902. (EL) BELOW: Pumping trials at Dotton Waterworks, 1909. Builder and brickmaker Thomas Abell is on the left. (EL)

The Exmouth Mercury.

A Weekly Newspaper, Directory, and Advertiser,

Circulating throughout Exmouth, Budleigh-Salterton, East Budleigh, Withycombe, Lympstone, Woodbury, &c.

| No. 457. | Registered for Transmission Abroad. | SATURDAY, FEBRUARY 4, 1865. | ONE PENNY. |

Exmouth Mercury.

THE PROSPECTS OF THE SESSION.

THE Session, now soon to be opened, seems likely to be about the dullest that will have been witnessed for many years past; it may be because it is the last of this Parliament, or, more likely, it results from the general prosperity of the nation at home, and from the prospect of peaceful external relations. This it is, too, that possibly will account for the evident apathy of the masses of the population on the question of reform itself—the only subject, indeed, which, by general consent, immediately affects them. And the American struggle, still vigorously prosecuted by both belligerents, having during its continuance caused every section of society to look on "with bated breath," has, perhaps, something to do in deadening our sensibility to the latter subject. Hence, in this also, may be found the primary motive, which has induced the section of extreme Liberals in Parliament, headed by Bright and Cobden, to feel all the greater necessity for strenuously impressing the question of reform on the public mind whensoever occasion offers. And, indeed, apart from the interest given in the vast number of recent speeches of statesmen and members of Parliament, from the Chancellor of the Exchequer downwards, the public mind has been rather cloyed than otherwise with the same accompaniment; and the strain of an eloquence that finds no immediate response among its several auditories. Under the guidance of a Government that has felt itself bound to secure for us progress at home, and which has shown itself zealous in withholding the country from foolish or unnecessary entanglement in foreign struggles, we may well rest thankful. While with these blessings at command, generous and unabated efforts are being made likewise for the advancement of general education, and our enlightened statesmen have taken the matter in hand to render the burden of taxation as light as possible for the masses. Recurring to these indubitable facts makes us believe that the coming Session must be altogether devoid of active interest. That there will, however, be interesting discussions, and possibly much speechifying throughout the term of the Session, is not to be questioned, as each member will be most anxious to show himself in the light of a useful representative in the eyes of his constituents, with a view to re-election whenever the present Parliament shall become defunct by a dissolution, it is most improbable, likewise, that either an extreme Liberal or Tory party—sections most unlikely to unite or fuse together, opposing principles and motives—shall be able to oust the present Ministry. The ordinary business of the country will, we presume, be all that shall be required of Government during the Session, and very probably here will be a spurt witnessed occasionally by some member or other ambitious of singularity. The malt tax may find a champion to ingratiate its mover with the ——— farming interests, and reform the ——— ——— crop up on one hand, with ——— necessity for in———

A rare copy of the *Exmouth Mercury*, 1865.

Exmouth in the 1880s, as the

s and the town improves.

The second issue of 'an amateur newspaper', the *Baring Press,* of
Exmouth, dated 1 March 1873, hitherto unrecorded. It was published
and printed by C. L. Wellsden at 2 Baring Place. (WG)

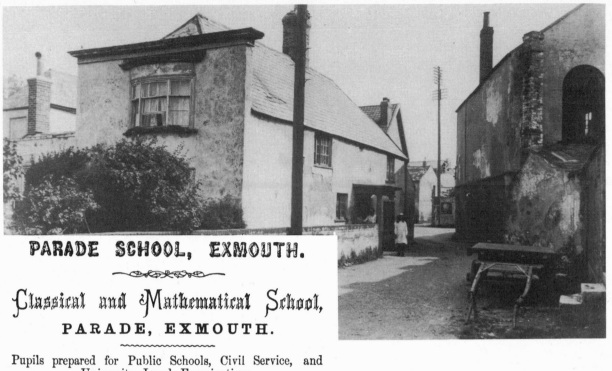

PARADE SCHOOL, EXMOUTH.

Classical and Mathematical School,
PARADE, EXMOUTH.

Pupils prepared for Public Schools, Civil Service, and University Local Examinations.

Eight Certificate Local Examinations; Two Civil Service Appointments, and One Scholarship, obtained since June, 1870.

References to Parents of present and past Pupils.

TERMS MODERATE.

MR. CHARLES SALTER, PRINCIPAL.

ABOVE: The School (left) in the 18th c. Elm Grove House on Manchester Quay (demolished 1938), and Balcony House (right) where the Magistrates once sat. (EL) CENTRE: Mr Charles Salter's Classical and Mathematical School, founded in 1846, still in business in 1872. BELOW: The pupils of the Ragged School in Ann Street line up in the 1890s. (LHNB)

ABOVE: The renowned Pencarwick School on the corner of Louisa Terrace in 1902, *alma mater* of Gen. Sir Redvers Buller, Adml. Sir Edward Chichester, Vice-Adml. Craigie, Lord Sidmouth's sons, and Lord Waleran. Closed in 1908. (LHNB) CENTRE: The Boarders' House, the Convent of the Holy Family, formerly 'Sunnyside'. (LHNB) BELOW: Today's Exmouth School — with 2,500 pupils, the largest comprehensive in England. (LHNB)

Lords and Commoners

A watering place with anything more than a seasonal reputation soon spawned large houses where the wealthy could accommodate not only their families, but a large retinue of servants. In 1828 it was lamented in Exmouth 'that no mansion sufficiently capacious for the reception of the Earl of Caernarvon and his numerous suite could be obtained', and his lordship duly decamped to a rival resort.

Marpool, Rill, Spratshays and Bystock, all mediaeval foundations, were the only large houses near the town until the 18th century. William Thomas Hull rebuilt Marpool, since demolished, early in the 19th century; Rill, the former home of Sir John Colleton, is long gone; Spratshays is an 18th century rebuilding after a fire, and Bystock dates only from 1907, having suffered a similar conflagration. The first house to reflect Exmouth's romantic attractions has also been swept away: Sacheveral Hall. Built about 1720 by Philip Bussel, it stood isolated on what is now Louisa Terrace and Louisa Place and in the mid-18th century passed into the hands of the wealthy Minifie family of Somerset clergymen, who used it as a periodic retreat from their mansion at Fairwater, near Taunton. It was a substantial three-storeyed house with stabling for twelve horses and by 1782 was held by Edward Iliff, a celebrated coaching proprietor, who died there at the age of 91 in 1819. The house was demolished soon after his death, so that a new 'crescent' of houses, started in 1822, could be built. It was named Louisa Terrace after Lord Rolle's second wife, whom he married in that year.

Few substantial houses were built in Littleham until after the Rolle Estate Act of 1865, but it was a different story in Withycombe. Here, builders sought the high ground and the romantic views across the estuary to the sea. Courtlands, named from the fields in which it lay, was probably built by the Barings in the late 18th century. They sold it to Lambert Blair and it was described in 1813 as an elegant mansion encircled by thriving plantations and gravel walks, with walled kitchen gardens, melon pits and hothouses. By 1819 it had been sold to Sir Walter Roberts, whose financial difficulties led to it being almost constantly up for sale between 1825 and 1828. Bought by William Francis Spicer in 1829, it was occupied by his family for many years.

East of Courtlands, below Woodbury Common, a three-storeyed house called Whimsey was built soon after 1785 by the eccentric John Freston Scrivenor (died 1797). He left it to his nephew because his daughter had married 'a damned parson' — the Bishop of Salisbury. Renamed Marley Lodge, because it stood in fields called the Marles, it passed through various hands, including those of General Broderick, until it was rebuilt in 1866 as Marley House. The new owner, John Pablo Bryce, had made a fortune trading in guano near Peru, and a great mansion was erected to the designs of C. P. Benmore. The Italian marble staircase alone cost £30,000. It stood, the grandest house that Exmouth ever saw, until its demolition in 1930.

Another 'whimsey', but one that fortunately survives, was A-la-Ronde. It was built in

1798, on former Hulham manor land purchased by Miss Jane Parminter in 1795 and is a miniature representation of the church of San Vitale at Ravenna, which Miss Jane and her cousin, Mary, evidently visited on their European travels. Originally thatched, its rooms were grouped round a central octagonal hall with shell gallery, which rose 60ft to a lantern above. There were no doors, but only vertically sliding panels. Because at high tide the ladies had to use a boat to reach Glenorchy Chapel, they built their own place of worship, Point-in-View, completed in 1811. The chapel was surrounded by a small school for six girls and almshouses for four maiden ladies aged over 50; a manse was added in 1829. Converted Jewesses were to be preferred for places in both almshouse and school, for the ladies considered the Jews to be God's chosen people and their return to the Holy Land dependent upon their conversion to Christianity. The famous requirement that the oaks on the estate should not be felled until the Jews had returned to Palestine does not appear, as frequently stated, in Miss Jane's will, but was probably a verbal tradition handed down in the district. It inspired the lines:

> 'List to the voice of the aged Trees,
> Pass them not heedless by;
> I hear in the sound of the moaning breeze
> The earnest and heartfelt cry
> Of her who willed that these trees should stand
> Till the Jews should return to the fatherland.'

Jane Parminter died in 1811 and her cousin Mary in 1849. A-la-Ronde was later occupied by a Parminter relation, the Rev Oswald Reichel (died 1923), in his day the foremost writer on the mediaeval history of Devon. His nieces, the Misses Tudor, lived in the house until recently.

Other notable houses included Bassett Park, built about 1850 for Charles Wheaton and sold in 1856 to Otho Cooke, who renamed it Withycombe House, and Rill Park, built by Thomas Burridge in 1856 and first occupied by the Rev J. T. Boles.

Exmouth owes its present form to the generosity and farsightedness of John, Baron Rolle of Stevenstone, who died at Bicton House on 3 April 1842, aged 85. He succeeded to the family estates, including Littleham manor, in 1797, on the death of his father, Dennys Rolle, and became the largest landowner in Devon. There was no public undertaking in the town which did not benefit from his largesse and the tradesmen held an annual dinner to celebrate his birthday. Incidentally, they repeatedly miscalculated his age, believing him to be six years older than in fact he was. In his youth he was Tory MP for Devon for 16 years, a staunch adherent of Pitt, but although he spoke frequently in the House he 'made no great figure as a debater'. In his latter years Greville described him as 'a choleric, hard-bitten old Tory'. His first wife, Judith, died in 1820 and two years later, at the age of nearly 66, he married the 25-year-old daughter of Lord Clinton, Louisa Barbara Trefusis. His estates, over 55,000 Devonshire acres, brought him £20,000 a year, but he lived modestly at an annual rate of about £5,000. His most embarrassing moment came when doing homage at the Coronation of Queen Victoria in 1838, as described in her diary. 'Poor old Lord Rolle, who is 82 and dreadfully infirm, in attempting to ascend the steps fell and rolled quite down, but was not the least hurt. When he attempted to re-ascend them, I got up and advanced to the end of the steps in order to prevent another fall.'

One commentator said of Rolle that 'his figure was handsome, as far as mere symmetry of limbs, and denied him all pretension to grace or elegance. Neither was his understanding apparently more cultivated than his manner was refined. He reminded me

126

always of a Devonshire rustic, but he possessed plain common sense, a manly mind, and the faculty of stating his ideas in a few strong words'. The locals remembered a conjuror called Moon who was employed as 'jester' to the noble lord when in one of his 'bad moods', and who occupied Upper West Down Farm from 1802. 'I can mind him coming into Exmouth', was one memory of Rolle. 'He was a big fellow and wore hob-nailed boots, and would come in damning and cursing everyone. They would just send and fetch Moon over to Bicton to quieten him. Moon was a regular wizard, and people do say he could cut the head off a cock and stick it on again.'

Rolle left no children, and the family property was bequeathed to his wife's five-year-old nephew, Mark George Kerr Trefusis, who took the surname Rolle. Lord Rolle's widow survived her husband for 43 years until 1885, and was in great demand for laying foundation stones and embarking on inaugural trips in successive lifeboats. There were great celebrations in the town when Mark Rolle came of age in 1856 and he continued much of his uncle's good work in the area. In particular his initials, M.R., can still be seen on the many farms and farm buildings which he rebuilt. In 1860 he married Gertrude Douglas, daughter of the Earl of Morton, after whom Gertrude Terrace, Morton Road and Crescent and Douglas Avenue were named. Mark Rolle died in 1907, and the manor of Littleham subsequently passed to his nephew, Lord Clinton (died 1957) and to the latter's great-grandson, the present Lord Clinton.

Many famous people have lived in the town; one was the landscape painter, Francis Danby. He came here in 1847, 'partly from taste and partly on the advice of his physician,' living first at Rill Cottage in North Street, adjoining the road since called Danby Terrace. Early in 1856 he moved into Shell House on the Maer. His paintings of the Exe estuary and its sunsets are well known, but he was also an accomplished amateur boat builder. He died here on 9 February 1861 and was buried at St John's in the Wilderness.

But it was not only the famous and the titled who enlivened Exmouth life over the years. There was the eccentric local rat catcher who, after a wager for two quarts of beer at the Dolphin Inn in 1823, ate two large rats, 'entrails and all', the first cooked, the second raw, and for another gallon offered to eat the landlord's tomcat if it could be caught for him. Then there was the Exmouth builder who fell victim to one of the first air disasters. John Fley had gone up to London for Queen Victoria's Coronation, but was killed by the premature descent of Mrs Graham's balloon in Marylebone Lane. A 'respectable tradesman' of the town paid £100 in 1850 to transport his wife and four children to the Californian Gold Rush — and actually arrived there. Mr Hull of Marpool Hall was fined 2s 6d for refusing to have his children vaccinated in 1860, after smallpox had raged in the town for several months. An anonymous local reporter of the same year had the temerity to comment on the annual picnic attended by 200 members of the Exmouth Temperance Society that 'the wet weather was a great disappointment, even to water drinkers'. George Foster, the grocer, discovered in his 'Exmouth Sauce' a rival to the more famous Worcestershire variety, and claimed in 1862 that it constituted 'an admirable adjunct to the luncheon and dinner table and was almost indispensable in the cuisine'. Without such characters, Exmouth would not have been Exmouth. Those were the credulous days when a child with whooping cough would be carried into a field while the dew was on the ground, a sleeping sheep sought out, moved and the child laid face down in its place.

Finally, imagine the reaction of the local postman faced in 1791 with a letter to deliver bearing the following address: 'Thisse heere lettur muste bee givinge bye the littal postboie thatt goes about with the Gentlemans letturs to Mr Winsor the Sun Meastur Shooemakur in the Neu Squire in the towne of Exmouth in the cowntee of Devonsheere'.

ABOVE: The shell of Bystock after the fire of 1906. (LHNB) BELOW:
Louisa Terrace, started 1822, seen from the sea in 1875, and showing the
New Road, now Carlton Hill. (LHNB)

Between SIR WALTER ROBERTS, Bart. and others   *Plaintiffs.*
SAMUEL ELYARD, and others - - - -   *Defendants.*

PARTICULARS

OF A VERY DESIRABLE

FREEHOLD ESTATE,

SITUATE

On the Eastern Bank of the River Exe, between Exmouth & Lympstone,

IN THE COUNTY OF DEVON,

Nine Miles distant from Exeter, and One from Exmouth;

CONSISTING OF

A CAPITAL FAMILY MANSION,

Called COURTLANDS,

ERECTED OF THE BEST MATERIALS, AND FINISHED IN A CHASTE & COSTLY MANNER;

CONTAINING

A handsome Entrance - Hall, elegant Drawing Rooms, and Library,

NUMEROUS AND WELL PROPORTIONED BED ROOMS, AND DRESSING ROOMS,

COACH HOUSES, STABLING, AND SUITABLE DOMESTIC OFFICES.

With Pleasure Grounds, Lawn, Flower Gardens, Plantations and Shrubberies, Conservatory,

PEACH HOUSES AND GRAPERY, GARDENS, WALLED ROUND,

AND SUNDRY ENCLOSURES OF PARK-LIKE LAND, STUDDED WITH TIMBER,

AND CONTAINING ABOUT

SIXTY-SIX ACRES.

THE MANSION is seated upon a gentle Eminence, at the extremity of a LAWN, protected on the North and East by full grown Plantations, and commands a View of its own Grounds, the RIVER EXE, the surrounding Country, and the SEA.

ALSO,

Two compact Freehold Farms, called Upper & Lower Halsdon,

Containing FORTY-SIX ACRES,

PRESENTING SEVERAL ELIGIBLE SITUATIONS FOR BUILDING.

Two Freehold Farms, called Higher & Lower Backenhayes,

Containing SIXTY-FIVE ACRES; AND

A SMALL FARM, called WATTONS, containing TWENTY ACRES.

𝕿𝖔 𝖇𝖊 𝕾𝖔𝖑𝖉,

Pursuant to a Decree and subsequent Order of the High Court of Chancery made in this Cause, with the approbation of

JOHN SPRINGETT HARVEY, ESQ.

One of the Masters of the said Court,

At the New London Inn, Exeter,

On MONDAY, the 26th Day of SEPTEMBER, 1825,

BETWEEN THE HOURS OF TWELVE AND ONE,

IN FOUR LOTS.

Particulars may be had gratis at the said Master's Chambers, in Southampton Buildings, Chancery Lane, London; of Mr. Barnes, Solicitor, at Exeter; of Mr. Zachary Turner, Solicitor, Exeter; at the Place of Sale; of Mr. Wm. Holt, Solicitor, Threadneedle Street; of Messrs. Oliverson and Denby, Solicitors, Frederick's Place, Old Jewry; and of Mr. Farebrother, Land Surveyor, &c. No. 6, Wellington Street, Strand, London. The Mansion and Grounds may be Viewed by applying on the Premises.

Courtlands on the market in 1825.

ABOVE: Courtlands today. (LHNB) CENTRE: Rich man's castle —
John Pablo Bryce's mansion, Marley House, 1866-1930. (EL) BELOW:
A-la-Ronde, the 'folly' of the cousins Parminter c1845. (WCSL)

130

ABOVE: 'Some Point in View, We all pursue' ran the couplet over the door of the Point-in-View Chapel (right); the Manse (left) was added in 1829. The picture was taken about 1845. (WCSL) CENTRE: Bassett Park, 1856. (EL) BELOW: The Manor House on Chapel Hill, demolished in 1894, showing Thomas Freeman's *Exmouth Journal* printing office and library (left). (EL)

'A choleric, hard-bitten old Tory'. Lord Rolle, creator of modern
Exmouth, as seen here by Cruikshank. (MC)

LEFT: Francis Danby, landscape painter. Bust by Christopher Moore, 1827. (NGI) RIGHT: The heir to 55,000 acres of Rolle estate, the Hon Mark George Kerr Rolle, d. 1907. (EL) BELOW: *Dead calm: sunset at the Bight of Exmouth* by Francis Danby, exhibited in London 1855. (LHNB)

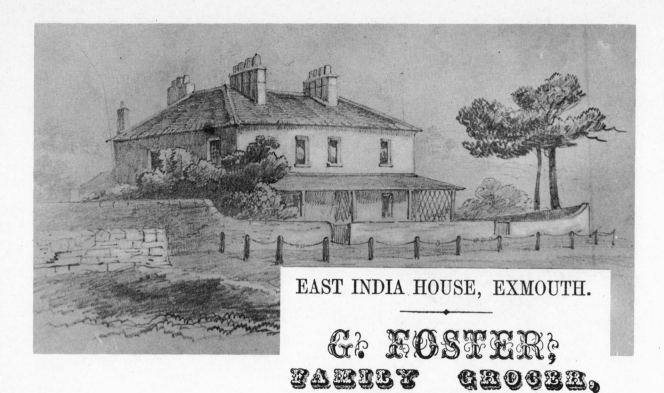

EAST INDIA HOUSE, EXMOUTH.

G. FOSTER,
FAMILY GROCER,
Wine Merchant,
AND
ITALIAN WAREHOUSEMAN.

Sole Agent for Garton's Prize Medal Ales.

ABOVE: Shell House, Danby's home on the Maer. (LHNB) BELOW: Where the ratcatcher ate an unorthodox meal: the Dolphin Hotel, 1930, demolished by enemy action 1941. (EL) INSET: George Foster, grocer of East India House (the site of Lennard's Bar on the Strand) and inventor of the 'Exmouth Sauce'.

Valete

Since my boyhood days in the Exmouth of the fifties, the town has grown out of all recogition. Surrounded on two sides by water, it could only expand to the north and east and thus the rapidity of its development seems all the greater. Both private and Council housing have bypassed Littleham village and advanced along the Budleigh road. Other estates have crawled steadily up St John's Road towards the church, often outstripping the shops and services which give some meaning to town life. The mediaeval Brixington Farm is now the Farmhouse Inn, ministering to a new generation of drinkers as thirsty as their forebears, its former farmlands submerged beneath a sea of red bricks. Since 1921 Exmouth's population has doubled, to pass 26,000. In the centre, one solitary thatched cottage survives in North Street.

The branch line to Budleigh Salterton and Sidmouth Junction, its first sod cut by Lady Gertrude Rolle a lifetime ago, along which one could travel to London with the milk churns, has been closed for more than a decade. The none-too-picturesque remnants of the old town in and around Market Street have been levelled and a new shopping centre is under construction. As I write, the much-needed relief road has been deferred, but will no doubt return, eventually to cut a new swathe through the town. Change is something to which we have grown accustomed, something to record before moving on. It costs little, nothing in fact, to pause occasionally and take a leisurely look back...

One of the men behind yesterday's cameras was James Sugg of the Station Parade — inviting custom in 1872. (EL)

Mr Sugg LEFT: offering studio scraps and entertainment in 1871, (EL) and RIGHT ABOVE: doing business in the Parade Gardens with his mobile darkroom. (LHNB) BELOW: Goods and people move up Carlton Hill in the late 19th century. (EL)

ABOVE: Grace and pace for the leisured classes, at Carlton House in the
1920s. (LHNB) BELOW: Benjamin Grigg and son take to the road —
Imperial Road in 1892. (LHNB)

137

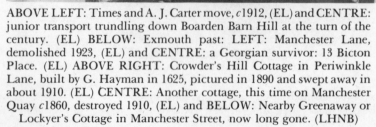

ABOVE LEFT: Times and A. J. Carter move, *c*1912, (EL) and CENTRE: junior transport trundling down Boarden Barn Hill at the turn of the century. (EL) BELOW: Exmouth past: LEFT: Manchester Lane, demolished 1923, (EL) and CENTRE: a Georgian survivor: 13 Bicton Place. (EL) ABOVE RIGHT: Crowder's Hill Cottage in Periwinkle Lane, built by G. Hayman in 1625, pictured in 1890 and swept away in about 1910. (EL) CENTRE: Another cottage, this time on Manchester Quay *c*1860, destroyed 1910, (EL) and BELOW: Nearby Greenaway or Lockyer's Cottage in Manchester Street, now long gone. (LHNB)

ABOVE: The 1897 Barn at Foxholes before its death by fire on 4 October 1905 and subsequent resurrection. Designed by E. S. Prior, it was called by Pevsner 'a brilliant exercise in Art Nouveau domestic design'. (LHNB)
BELOW: Queen's Court partly survives; some of it came down in 1939. (LHNB)

ABOVE: A corner of the Strand c1860, with the Post Office on the left —
now Lloyds Bank. (LHNB) CENTRE: Strand enclosure c1910. (EL)
BELOW: Exmouth still changes. Staple's Buildings off the Parade, built
by Abraham Staple in 1810, pictured immediately before demolition in
late June 1977. (LHNB)

ABOVE: Exmouth Central Area Redevelopment Scheme (which included Staple's Buildings) due for completion in 1979. (LHNB) CENTRE: Bicton Street survives intact, representing an older Exmouth now once again fashionable. (LHNB) BELOW: Marine Drive at Orcombe Point in the seventies — an escape for 20th century Britons. (LHNB)

Bibliography and Sources

Adams, E., *Francis Danby: Varieties of Poetic Landscape* (1973)

Brabazon, E. J., *Exmouth and its Environs* (1866)

Calendars of Charter, Close, Fine, and Patent Rolls

Calendar of the Committees for Compounding and Advance of Money

Calendars of Inquisitions Post Mortem, Papal Registers, and State Papers Domestic

Cann, I. G., *Exmouth History* (1967-77) (typescript)

Chope, R. P. (ed), *Early Tours in Devon and Cornwall* (1918)

Chown, C. E., and J. P. Morris, *The Story of Exmouth Lifeboats* (1974)

Clark, E. A. G., *The Ports of the Exe Estuary* (1960) (and his thesis)

Contact, Withycombe Raleigh parish magazine (articles by W. G. N. Gorfin)

Delderfield, E. R., *Exmouth Milestones* (1948); *Exmouth Yesterdays* (1952)

Devon and Cornwall Notes and Queries (1900-   )

Devon and Cornwall Record Society (1905-   )

Devonshire Domesday and Geld Inquest (1884-92)

Directories of Devon and Exmouth (various, 1824 to date)

Exmouth Ancient and Modern (1868)

Farr, G., *Wreck and Rescue on the Coast of Devon* (1968)

Glenorchy Congregational Church (1963)

Goodall, J. L., *One Hundred Years and More* (1963)

Gover, Mawer and Stenton, *Place Names of Devon* (1931-2)

Hingeston Randolph, F. C. (ed), *Registers of the Diocese of Exeter* (1886-1915)

Historical Manuscripts Commission, *Records of Exeter Corporation* (1912)

Hoskins, W. G., *Devon* (1954), with H. P. R. Finberg, *Devonshire Studies* (1952)

Letters and Papers of Henry VIII

Lysons, D., *Magna Britannia, Devon* (1822)

Oliver, G., *Monasticon Dioecesis Exoniensis* (1846)

Oppenheim, M. M., *The Maritime History of Devon* (1968)

Pole, Sir W., *Collections of the History of Devon* (1791)

Polwhele, R., *History of Devon* (1793-1806)

Sheldon, G., *From Trackway to Turnpike* (1928)

Stirling, A. M. W., *The Ways of Yesterday* (1930)

Transactions of the Devonshire Association (1863-   )

Webb, W., *Memorials of Exmouth* (1872) (and 2nd edn. as W. Everitt, 1885)

Also: *Complete Peerage, Dictionary of National Biography, Gentleman's Magazine*

Extensive use has been made of manuscript sources in the Devon Record Office, particularly the Rolle Estate Papers, which include the hundred rolls of East Budleigh and the manorial records of Littleham. The parish records of both Littleham and Withycombe have proved indispensable. Records of the ferry are among the Exeter City Muniments and early educational material is held with the Diocesan Records. Other manuscripts consulted include the Cartulary of St Nicholas' Priory in the British Museum, Littleham records in Exeter Cathedral Library, court rolls and surveys of Wode *iuxta* Chickstone in the Somerset Record Office (Trevelyan papers) and subsidy and other rolls in the Public Record Office.

145

146

Subscribers

Presentation copies

1 Exmouth Town Committee
2 East Devon District Council
3 Exmouth Branch Library
4 Exmouth Historical & Archaeological Society
5 The Rt Hon Lord Clinton JP
6 Cllr D. E. Dray

7 Robin Bush
8 Clive Birch
9 Jeffrey Nicholas Bowden
10 Mrs E. Barlow
11 R. M. Jones
12 I. G. Cann
13 J. Dale
14 Owen E. Roberts
15 Mrs Holmes-Edge
16 L. A. Hallett
17 Mrs I. E. Buer
18 Mrs Lilian Anderson
19 Miss E. M. Supple
20 Mrs M. D. Corder
21 Mrs S. Molland
22 Miss Y. C. O. Caselli
23 L. Hill
24 Miss M. V. Sedgwick
25 F. Smith
26 G. E. Wheeler
27 Mrs Iris M. Bush
28 Miss Sue Hull
29 M. Pendry
30 A. J. Grace
31 R. D. Ison
32 Joan B. Maden
33 G. P. Schofield
34 Lindsay & James Gorman
35 Mr Eric & Mrs Jean Frost
36 Peter Chard
37 Mrs W. E. Holley
38 Mrs Jo Jackson
39 H. O. Davies
40 A. W. M. Ayling
41 Dickson Tolman
42 Robin Ann Reffell
43 G. Billington
44 J. Fowler
45 Frederick & Moya Bush
46 Angela Field
47 Miss Margaret S. Hayman
48 P. D. Clapp
49 Glyn Pope
50 Mrs O. F. Marshall
51 Miss V. I. Ellis
52 Enid I. Floyd
53 Mrs J. B. Jowitt
54 Miss P. E. Bardens
55 G. D. Shutter
56 Mrs T. Holbrook
57 Mrs Mary L. Browning
58 Michael L. Browning
59 Capt I. H. Jackson BEM
60 Mrs D. M. Lee
61 Mrs Philip Scott
62 Mrs H. Moorhouse
63 Miss C. C. Dixon
64 Peter Turner
65 A. R. Gossington
66 Mayd Radford
67 Jeremy Duncan
68 Mrs Josephine M. Payne
69 Mrs Lynne Elizabeth Howe
70 Mrs H. G. Baker
71 Miss R. Kemeys-Jenkin
72 Mrs A. Dixon
73 Mrs M. Martin
74 Miss Zambra
75 R. Tootell
76 Mr & Mrs L. M. Lees
77 Miss Margaret Hallett
78 R. T. Dimond
79 B. H. Marchant
80 Derrick E. Dray

81 Mr & Mrs Douglas Paling
82 D. C. Pethybridge
83 Paul T. Pearson
84 Mr & Mrs J. Spittel
85 The Royal Beacon Hotel
86 Robert Squire
87 D. R. Redgwell
88 Thomas Adams Roseveare
89 G. F. T. Pickard
90 Mrs A. L. Bennett
91 Mrs Wilson
92 J. Hayward
93 Mary Ann Davis
94 Miss M. W. Hodder
95 Mrs C. Mogford
96 David W. West
97 Miss J. F. Newcombe
98 Mrs P. Wilkinson
99 Mrs R. M. Price
100 Anne Scott
101 W. E. Rosenfeld
102 Mrs B. L. Wood
103 Mrs E. Pym
104
106 Mrs W. Ellett
107 Mrs J. R. Edwardes-Ker
108
112 Eagle Investments Ltd
113 K. Edwards
114 B. P. Tranter
115 R. J. Linley
116 R. Hole
117 M. J. Fagan
118 W. F. Mulcahy
119 G. L. Brewster
120 Mrs I. S. Hosegood
121 A. E. Hobbis
122 K. M. McKay
123 David C. Gossington
124 Mrs B. Forshaw
125 Mr & Mrs R. G. L. Benzie
126 Mrs K. Wood
127 Dr Rodney L. Horder
128 Miss L. Smalley
129 Miss Hilda I. Grimmer
130
131 Mrs P. J. Styler
132 J. O. Shewring
133 Miss D. I. Axon
134 Mr & Mrs L. Pike
135 F. Williams
136 Mrs J. G. Chalk
137 G. D. Perkins
138 Dr & Mrs Gordon Flint
139 John D. G. McCrae
140 Mrs Maureen K. Bailey
141 Mrs M. Laithwaite
142 P. T. Bays
143 John E. Beeston

144 Mrs Clare Oliver
145 Mrs Nancy Thompson
146 Dr L. J. Marshall
147 Judith Floyd
148 P. J. Hartnell
149 B. J. Perry BSc
150 Mrs M. Lazell
151 R. Payne
152 Mrs Edith Edwards
153 B. D. Chave
154 C. H. C. Pope
155 Rev C. M. Grail
156 Miss E. M. Sharman
157 Mr & Mrs A. C. Goodwin
158 Miss F. Vibert
159 Mrs G. J. Bradford
160 C. J. Blazey
161 Miss G. N. Ellis
162 John Burt
163 A. C. Goodwin MA
164 L. E. Downes
165 D. Fisher
166 Mildred Louise Hayne
167 G. A. Hyman
168 Mrs Anne Hampson
169 F. G. Tupman
170 N. L. Stevens
171 Miss L. E. Henderson
172 Miss I. Boyes
173 Miss K. Hadley
174 W. G. Broom
175 D. W. Carter
176 L. E. Kingdon
177 Miss M. J. Henshaw
178 Mr & Mrs James Vardy
179 Mrs Christine Field
180 Mr & Mrs J. Forte
181 Graham Bastin
182 Philip V. Darch
183 W. H. Gillott
184 Mrs J. Wheeler
185 Mrs E. Jones
186 Mrs Marjorie Budd
187 Mrs R. Prall
188 Mrs M. Herbert
189 Rev George Whitfield
190 Miss B. Hallett
191 R. Hallett
192 Mrs M. Scott
193 Mrs M. Deggim
194 Mrs A. Hatton
195 P. A. Hatton
196 Peter Letten
197 L. H. Glisson
198 Miss P. Dawn J. Stevens
199 Mrs J. Lord
200 Exmouth Library
201 Mrs J. Glaister
202 Mrs Marilyn J. Toye
203 Mrs W. R. Hellier
204 M. D. Rendell
205 W. J. Stradling

206 Simon R. Jenkinson
207 G. E. Crewe
208 D. C. Fieldsend
209 Mrs K. M. Turner
210 Robert C. W. Skidmore
211 Mr & Mrs D. F. Stevens
212 C. D. Finch
213 Miss C. Jenkins
214 Mrs Betty Cleave
215 Dorothy Cox
216 Mr & Mrs G. H. L. Nickells
217 Mr & Mrs G. H. L. Hellier
218 R. Squire
219 J. Heland
220 Dr J. O. P. Edgcumbe
221 G. Dymond
222 D. Adams
223 Bob Missen
224 R. E. Harvey
225 E. J. Paget
226 P. T. Dixon
227 Simon R. Jenkinson
228 Mrs F. L. E. Manser
229 Mrs J. Liddle
230 Edwin S. Putt
231 E. A. W. Ledbury
232 Mrs B. R. Bowen
233 H. A. Pulford
234 Miss J. M. Key
235 Mrs I. D. King
236 J. E. Price
237 Mrs Thelma Wills
238 J. S. Woolgar
239 B. G. Burnett
240 M. Oldham
241 T. A. Judge
242 J. C. White
243 Judith Grant
244 T. V. Uren
245 D. R. Cosway
246 Geoffrey William Gooding
247 Charles Norman Drew
248 Terence Moger
249 P. F. Zubka-Grant
250 E. F. W. Grant
251 Mrs M. W. Rubbins
252 A. Sayers
253 Mrs L. C. Wellington
254 Mrs R. Cordin
255 Mrs A. Amos
256 Carol Buckler
257 Mrs P. Olwer
258 L. G. Sansom
259 T. J. Pitman
260 Janet Wimbush
261 Mr & Mrs K. E. Croft
262 E. W. Smith
263 N. R. London
264 T. G. Collins
265 Miss Joan Oldham
266 E. M. Richardson
267 M. Townsend
268 Mrs M. D. Morriss
269 Mrs M. M. Johnston
270 Mrs B. Smeath
271 K. L. Moass
272 Mrs I. Pearson
273 F. Hall
274 Mr & Mrs D. Bown
275 G. W. Fardell
276 F. Gray
277 Mr & Mrs J. E. Powles
278 E. F. Bird
279 Mrs J. A. Parker
280 Mrs Shelagh P. M. Hughes

281 Mrs Shirley Wilkes
282 D. E. Murch
283 Jonathan Eeward Pawsey
284 A. G. Morris
285 Brian L. Dempster
286 Mrs B. Wood
287 Mrs D. Fuller
288 Miss J. L. Palmer
289 R. R. & A. Nott
290 Miss P. M. Carter
291 Mrs I. F. Thomas
292 Mr & Ms M. T. Fairclough
293 Mrs Drecka
294 Mrs Sandra Maclure
295 G. S. Mathews
296 R. W. J. Mellish
297 Mrs H. M. Leeman
298 J. K. Ware
299 F. W. Geall
300 Charles H. Tufnell
301 M. J. C. Shepherd
302 Leslie W. Aplin
303 Kenneth Malcolm Medley
304 Mrs G. M. Bassett
305 Dorothy & Roland Rogers
306 William John Braddick
307 John R. Rowsell
308
309 Mrs M. V. Greenham
310 L. G. Jerram
311 Henry Charles Francis
312 C. V. Lucas
313 Mrs M. M. Burdett
314 Dr R. W. Covill
315 Mrs Anne Rix
316 M. Rendall
317 Mrs L. E. Partridge
318 Misses V. & G. Smalridge
319 B. Doble
320 Mr & Mrs P. Travers
321 R. S. Bagshaw (Exmouth Town Clerk 1956-74)
322 Vernon B. Pye (lately Devon County Councillor)
323 A. H. D. Spencer
324 Anthony Bell Forster
325 E. Norton
326 Mrs M. Crutchley
327 Mrs L. D. Norton
328 Mrs E. Webber
329 M. Webber
330 W. Taylor
331 W. A. Hermitage
332 Betty Clench Mundy
333 Mrs Barbara M. Miners
334 Bruce Richard Peeke
335 William George Bamsey
336 Mrs Hazel Doreen Logan

337 Lynnette May Pritchard
338 J. D. Warburton
339 M. H. Stamp
340 Peter King
341 R. M. Owen
342 G. J. Fox
343 Phil Ousley
344 Mrs Ann Hughes
345 J. R. Bowley
346 G. Hudson
347 Mrs P. Jones
348 MRS M. Matheson
349 Peter Morey
350 Mrs H. J. Kaczmarek
351 W. Pyne
352 M. A. Jovcic
353 R. G. Moffat
354 Mrs J. Hockney
355 Mrs J. A. Russell
356 J. Stagg
357 Mrs M. A. Douglass
358 Terence Jones
359 Dave Westaway
360 S. R. Weightman
361 Mrs A. O. Roberts
362 Mrs P. J. Moss
363 Mrs B. J. Marston
364 L. C. J. Litton
365 J. C. Garwood
366 R. J. Preston
367 Mrs D. Parker
368 Emeritus Professor P. J. Stoy
369 Miss Monica Cole
370 Mr & Mrs R. Green
371 Mrs W. Shapter
372 Mrs D. M. H. Barraclough
373 S. R. Skidmore
374 Mr & Mrs Ashton Kidder
375 Mr & Mrs John Harvey
376 T. J. Hill
377 D. A. Brooks
378 Mrs J. Maunder
379 Miss C. Knight
380 Miss P. M. George
381 John Onley
382 D. G. Abbott
383 C. W. Steedman
384 Alan F. Goodwin
385 Mrs Willmot
386 Paul Butler
387 Mrs S. Sansom
388 M. C. Packenham
389 George Friday
390 Mrs Pearcy
391 Mrs Joan Hawkins
392 Charles Rockett
393 C. P. Stone
394 Quentin Earle
395 Miss Valerie L. Roper
396 R. W. J. Mills

397 Devon & Exeter Institution Library
398 Miss D. M. Bradbeer
399 Miss A. Meaden
400 Mrs A. A. D. Hacking
401 Mrs Hore
402 Kelly Baggley
403 T. C. Buckingham
404 Jim & Marjorie Cummings
405 Kenneth Proctor
406 Mrs Priscilla Hull
407 Fairlynch Arts Centre & Museum
408 Miss E. R. Perrian
409 Mrs V. Grose
410 Mrs M. F. Beatty
411 W. Urquhart
412 Mrs J. E. Tiller
413 Nellie Board
414 Joyce Walsh
415 Mrs. C. M. Rice
416 Catherine Bush
417 Alexander Bush
418 Mrs I. M. Sanders
419 W. G. Owen
420
422 Mrs A. S. Ratcliffe
423 Raymond Hill
424 Mrs June Binkert
425 Rev Canon J. G. Barnish
426 J. & S. Blanchard
427 A. J. Jones
428 P. L. & S. A. Haycox
429 James Stagg
430 W. E. Needham
431 Exeter College
432 Messrs John W. Palmer
433 Roy G. Richards
434 Mr & Mrs R. L. Pearcy
435 Mrs C. Keay
436 W. Gorfin
437 R. J. Chapman
438 Marpool C. P.
439 School
440 Steven Pitts
441 Lester Smith
442 M. J. Huggins
443
444 Rentex Vehicle Hire
445 Meadows & Co.
446 R. F. Chapple
447
449 Rolle College
450 Mrs V. Brice
451 Susan Brown
452 Carlton Lodge Hotel
453 Mrs H. Jones
454 Mrs Sylvia Mary Willis
455 N. J. Batten
456 D. J. Dawkins
457 A. K. B. Ede

458 Edwin Chappell
459 Peter H. Thorpe
460 Exmouth Amusement
461 Centre
462 Seaforth Hotel
463 Exmouth Teachers' Centre
464 A. G. Tuckett
465 John Onley
466 The Barn Hotel
467 Exmouth School
468 Richard A. L. Waller
469 Gordon & Priscilla
474 Hull
475 M. B. Saunders
476 J. A. Orchard
477 K. E. Croft
478 R. J. Clough
479 L. D. Cady
480 John T. Hawkins
481 Michael J. Maine
482 J. C. de V. Roberts
483 K. Goodridge
484 Rev Canon F. G. Rice
485 Devon Record Office
486 Miss Joyce Packe
487 T. L. G. Landon
488 Mrs U. W. Brighouse
489 N. L. P. Smith
490 J. L. Jervose
491 Mrs C. D. Lineham
492 Cecil Tapscott Mason
493 R. E. Wilson
494 J. D. Pidgeon
495 Michael J. Egerton
496 A. J. Hutchings
497 R. W. A. Guiver
498 Charles William Beckerleg
489 C. F. Retter
500 St Luke's College
501 George Tremlett
502 B. J. Fisher
503 A. D. Tucker
504 P. B. M. Josephson
505 Mrs M. M. Gilpin
506 Richard Webb
507 Dr J. R. Andrews
508 Field Marshall Sir Richard Hull
509 H. M. Cope
510
529 Devon County Library
530 Victoria & Albert Museum
531 David Read
532 Malcolm Read
533 John Walker
534 Stephen & Vicki Wegg-Prosser
535 Joan & Tony Lammiman

(Remaining names unlisted.)

KEY TO CAPTION CREDITS

EL   Thomas Abell Reference Library, Exmouth
LHNB   Leslie Hill and Nigel Batten
NGI   National Gallery of Ireland
WG   W. G. N. Gorfin
WCSL   West Country Studies Library, Exeter

ENDPAPERS: FRONT — Exmouth in its context, 1765. BACK — Exmouth c1840.

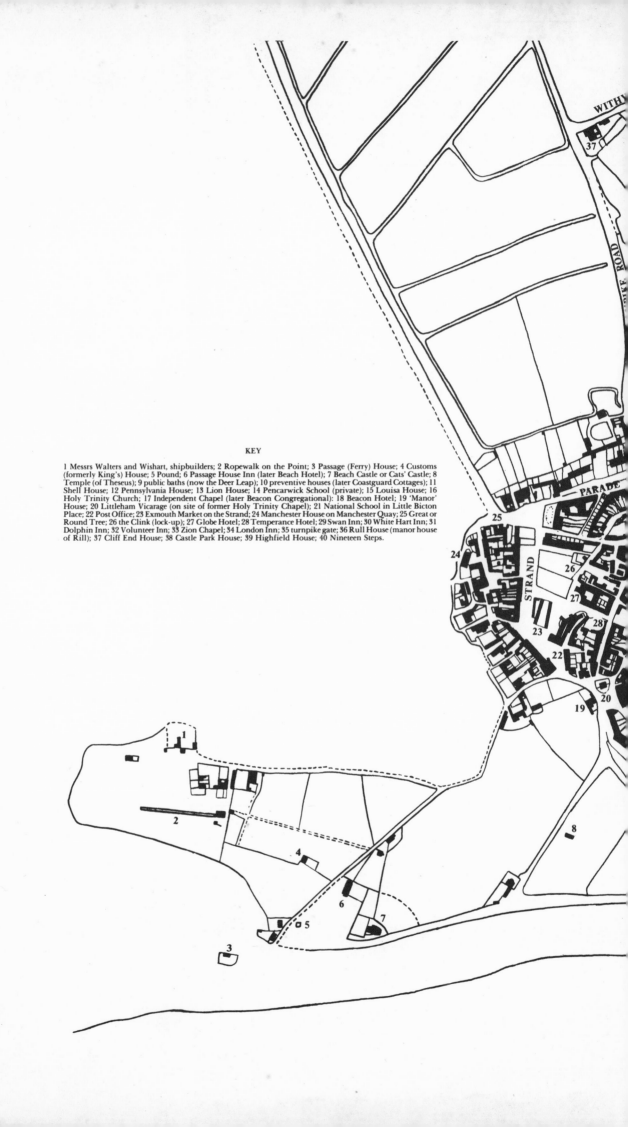

KEY

1 Messrs Walters and Wishart, shipbuilders; 2 Ropewalk on the Point; 3 Passage (Ferry) House; 4 Customs (formerly King's) House; 5 Pound; 6 Passage House Inn (later Beach Hotel); 7 Beach Castle or Cats' Castle; 8 Temple (of Theseus); 9 public baths (now the Deer Leap); 10 preventive houses (later Coastguard Cottages); 11 Shell House; 12 Pennsylvania House; 13 Lion House; 14 Pencarwick School (private); 15 Louisa House; 16 Holy Trinity Church; 17 Independent Chapel (later Beacon Congregational): 18 Beacon Hotel; 19 'Manor' House; 20 Littleham Vicarage (on site of former Holy Trinity Chapel); 21 National School in Little Bicton Place; 22 Post Office; 23 Exmouth Market on the Strand; 24 Manchester House on Manchester Quay; 25 Great or Round Tree; 26 the Clink (lock-up); 27 Globe Hotel; 28 Temperance Hotel; 29 Swan Inn; 30 White Hart Inn; 31 Dolphin Inn; 32 Volunteer Inn; 33 Zion Chapel; 34 London Inn; 35 turnpike gate; 36 Rull House (manor house of Rill); 37 Cliff End House; 38 Castle Park House; 39 Highfield House; 40 Nineteen Steps.